READY**SET** STITCH

LEARN TO DECORATE FABRICS WITH 20 HOT PROJECTS

SUSIE JOHNS AND CAROLINE SMITH

Creative Publishing
international

Creative Publishing
international

First published in the USA and Canada in 2007 by
Creative Publishing international, Inc.
18705 Lake Drive East
Chanhassen Minnesota 55317
1-800-328-3895
www.creativepub.com
All rights reserved

President/CEO: Ken Fund
VP Sales & Marketing: Peter Ackroyd
Executive Managing Editor: Barbara Harold
Creative Director: Michele Lanci-Altomare
Production Managers: Laura Hokkannen, Linda Halls

First published in UK in 2007 by
Carroll & Brown Publishers
20 Lonsdale Road
Queens Park
London NW6 6RD

Photographer: Jules Selmes

Copyright © Carroll & Brown Publishers Limited 2007

Library of Congress Cataloging-in-Publication Data

Johns, Susie.
Ready, set, stitch : learn thand and machine embroidery techniques with
20 hot projects / Susie Johns & Caroline Smith.
p. cm.
Includes index.
ISBN-13: 978-1-58923-343-0 (soft cover)
ISBN-10: 1-58923-343-3 (soft cover)
1. Embroidery--Patterns. 2. Embroidery, Machine. I. Smith, Caroline,
1961- II. Title.

TT771.J625 2007
746.44'041--dc22   2007003471

Printed in China

10 9 8 7 6 5 4 3 2 1

CONTENTS

INTRODUCTION

Ready, set, stitch! In no time, you'll be making fabulous accessories, garments, and household items or transforming already owned plainer versions into something really special. Embroidery, whether by hand or machine, is so easy to do, you'll wonder why you waited so long to get stitching.

Hand embroidery has a long and venerable history. Since the earliest times, people have wanted to embellish their clothes and other items – perhaps to set themselves apart or to make use of innate creativity. Dozens of different stitches were developed in order to translate these desires into reality. In this book, you'll find a wide range to help you recreate what you want to capture.

Different regions produced different styles of embroidery, too, such as drawn threadwork, cutwork, and smocking, Their decorative potentials expanded how plain fabric could be transformed into something unique. Again, using this book, you will be able to master these techniques and create attractive projects on which to practice.

More recently, sewing machines have brought a new dimension to decorative stitching – speed. Even with the simplest of machines, you can embellish items with colorful borders and motifs. In this book, you'll also learn about freehand design, which can produce all-over patterns.

For hand embroidery, little in the way of equipment is required – a needle and some embroidery floss. And, it's very portable so you can practice wherever you have a place to sit and good lighting – outdoors, in waiting rooms, etc. – as well as at home. As mentioned previously, to produce decorative effects and the projects in this book, all you need is a basic sewing machine .

The book has been designed to teach you all the basic stitching techniques and inspire you to use them through 20 original projects. The garments, accessories, and household items that are included have been created so that even novice needleworkers can achieve a successful result. They also demonstrate how variable are the looks and uses of stitching, and they should prove enjoyable to wear or use or to give as gifts.

Susie Johns

Caroline Smith

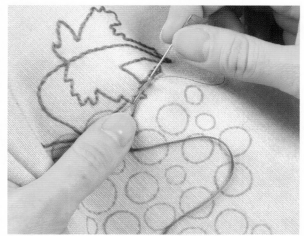

HAND EMBROIDERY

Needle and thread can produce the most wonderful effects on fabric. With just simple cross stitch you can create all kinds of letters and images while knotted, flat, and looped stitches will produce life-like renditions of practically anything you can dream up. Smocking, cutwork, and drawn, and pulled threadwork manipulate the basic fabric, producing decorative material, while beadwork can add sparkle and texture. In this chapter, you will find all the techniques you need to master these skills — and more — plus over a dozen delightful items to wear and use.

Tools and materials

Embroidery can be done successfully on most fabrics and the wide range of threads available means you can achieve many different effects. Your only other essential piece of equipment, outside of a needle, is a small, sharp pair of scissors.

EMBROIDERY THREADS
These come in a wide range of colors. Among the most popular types are:

Embroidery floss a loosely twisted 6-strand thread that is easily divided into single threads.

Pearl cotton a strong, twisted non-divisible thread with a high sheen.

Flower thread a fine non-divisible thread with a matt finish.

Matt embroidery cotton a thick, soft, tightly twisted thread.

Crewel yarn fine 2-ply wool or acrylic yarn.

Persian yarn loosely twisted and easily divisible 3-strand wool or acrylic yarn.

NEEDLES
These come in a wide range of sizes; the higher the number the finer the needle. The most useful ones (shown opposite) are described below.

Crewel or embroidery needle the most commonly used embroidery needle. It has a sharp point and a large eye.

Chenille needle similar to a crewel needle but with a thicker stem. It is suitable for working with heavier threads on a coarse background fabric.

Tapestry or yarn needle a thick-stemmed, large-eyed needle with a round-pointed end. Used for lacing embroidery stitches and for pulled threadwork.

Beading needle a fine, long needle for sewing on tiny beads.

OTHER EQUIPMENT
Pairs of large and small sharp scissors for cutting your fabric and thread are absolutely essential. You'll also want dressmaker's carbon paper and special pencils for transferring your embroidery designs to fabric. Other useful items include a thimble, needle threader, and masking tape to prevent fabric edges from fraying.

FABRICS

Both plain or patterned fabrics are suitable for embroidery. A wide range of even-weave fabrics for counted-thread techniques (such as cross stitch) is available. This has the same number of warp and weft threads per square inch. One of the most popular is 14 count Aida cloth.

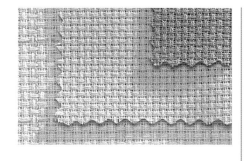

This is also available with a woven colored grid to make stitch counting from charts easier. The colored threads are removed when the stitching is finished.

Each project in this book contains a description of suitable fabrics, but when you start creating your own pieces, keep in mind that the fabric should be suitable for the finished item – for example, hardwearing and washable for a cushion cover.

CUTTING AND BINDING FABRIC

The fabric should be cut 2" (5 cm) larger all around than the overall design. But if you want to mount or frame the completed embroidery, (see page 93) add twice this amount – 4" (10 cm). Take care to cut the fabric straight, following the warp and weft threads of the weave of the fabric.

Binding fabric prevents the edges from fraying while you work and is essential on loosely woven fabric. Either tape the edges with masking tape or neaten raw edges with machine zigzag stitch. Alternatively, turn the edges under and sew in place.

THREADS

USING THREADS

The working thread should be 18" (45 cm) or less. Longer threads will get tangled, lose their sheen, and fray. It's a good idea to cut skeins into lengths before you start. Fold bundles in half widthwise, and tie a thread around the loop end. Use as needed.

Don't make a knot when starting or finishing a length of thread; knots show through the work and create an uneven appearance. Instead, use a small backstitch (see page 17), or weave the end into existing stitches on the back of the work. Try to keep the back of the work as neat as possible by weaving the thread ends behind existing stitches and avoiding large gaps between stitches.

SECURING THREADS

1 Start a new thread by sliding the needle under the wrong side of some of the stitches, keeping the thread end about 1½" (4 cm) long. Bring the needle up on the right side of the fabric and continue.

2 At the end of stitching, secure the thread by sliding the needle under 1½" (4 cm) of the worked stitches on the wrong side of the work, and then cut the thread.

Working with a frame

Frames hold the fabric taut while you work. A frame isn't essential for small pieces of embroidery, but it does make the work easier to handle and quicker to stitch. With a frame, the fabric is held at an even tension so the stitches themselves will be more even. Also, by holding the frame instead of the fabric, this keeps the work cleaner than working without one.

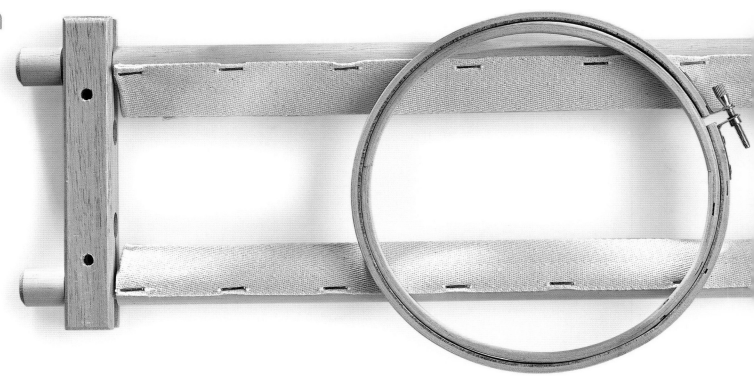

There are two basic types of frame: the round frame or hoop and the straight-sided frame. The hoop is the most commonly used because it is lightweight and portable, and it only takes a few seconds to correctly mount the fabric in it. Hoops are made of wood, metal, or plastic, and come in a variety of sizes, ranging from 5-10" (12.5- 25 cm) in diameter. The frame has two hoops that are placed one inside the other, stretching the fabric between them. The outer hoop opens, and has a screw to adjust the tension.

Straight-sided frames, known as stretcher frames, are generally used for large pieces of embroidery such as wall hangings because they stretch the work very evenly. A frame usually consists of four pieces of wood, with a roller at the top and bottom to which strips of webbing are nailed. Two flat sides fit into the rollers and are secured by pegs or screws. It takes longer to mount the work in a stretcher frame, but the fabric is quickly moved into a new position. Both types of frames are available on floor or lap stands, which allow you to keep both hands free.

WORKING WITH A HOOP

Before placing the fabric, loosen the tension screw on the outer hoop. The hoop can be repositioned on the fabric as you complete each small area of stitching.

1 Lay the fabric on top of the inner hoop, with the section to be embroidered facing you.

2 Make sure that the fabric is smooth. Push the outer hoop down on top of the fabric on the inner hoop. Gently pull the fabric taut. Tighten the upper hoop by turning the screw, so that the fabric is stretched like a drum and held firmly in position.

IRREGULARLY SHAPED WORK
Baste the irregular shape onto a larger piece of fabric, with the woven threads of each aligned.
 Mount the fabric in the usual way. Cut away the supporting fabric on the wrong side of the shape so that it is ready to embroider.

WORKING WITH A FRAME

Before you mount the fabric, hem all the edges, or bind them with ¾" (2 cm) wide cotton tape. Mark the center point of the fabric on the top and bottom edges.

1 Match the center points on the rollers and fabric, and work from the center. Herringbone stitch the edges of the fabric to the roller webbing.

2 Slot the sides into the rollers, and pull the fabric tight by adjusting the frames. Lace the sides of the fabric loosely to the frame using strong thread. Tighten the thread on both sides. Adjust the frame and secure with firm knots.

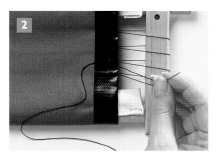

PROTECTING YOUR WORK
You can bind your hoop to prevent fine fabrics sagging and losing their shape while you work. For a large piece of embroidery, change the hoop position every time a section is complete.
 Wrap woven tape around the inner hoop, and secure the end with a few stitches. Place the fabric on the lower hoop and lay white tissue paper on top. Mount the fabric and paper, then tear away the paper.
 When you reposition your work, be sure to protect the finished stitches with a layer of tissue paper.

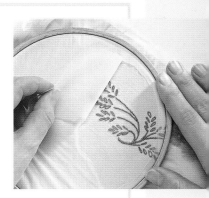

Inspiration for embroidery designs can be found almost anywhere. Start by looking at old embroidery, art postcards, photographs, book illustrations, or wallpaper.

You can find ideas for designs from many different items, including plates, tiles, and natural objects such as shells, and flora, and fauna. Antique objects often have attractive decorations that could easily be copied for embroidery designs.

Since the original design is unlikely to be the right size, you will need to enlarge or reduce it to suit. The easiest way to do this is with a photocopier – you simply keep enlarging (or reducing) your design, remembering, when enlarging, to change to A3 paper, if necessary.

Alternatively, you can use the grid method shown below. This involves transposing the outline shapes of the basic design from one grid to another of a different size. You will need some good quality tracing paper, a ruler, and a set square. If a design has a lot of detail, try to simplify the outlines to suit the scale of your work.

With cross-stitch designs, each stitch fills a small square. Designs can be worked out in grid form using graph paper, and shading the squares with colored pencils.

TO ENLARGE A DESIGN

1 Trace shapes on tracing paper, and go over all lines with a black felt-tip pen. Enclose the design in a rectangle. Draw a diagonal line from the bottom left-hand corner to the top right-hand corner.

2 Place the traced rectangle on a sheet of paper large enough for the final design. Align the left-hand and bottom edges. Tape down the tracing; extend the diagonal line on the tracing across the paper.

3 Remove the paper and complete the diagonal line. At the height of the new design, using a set square, draw a horizontal line to cross the diagonal. From this point, draw a vertical line down to bottom edge.

4 Divide the original tracing into equal squares. Draw the same number of squares on the paper enlargement. Copy the lines in the small squares on the tracing paper to the equivalent large squares on the paper by marking the points where the design lines intersect the grid and join them.

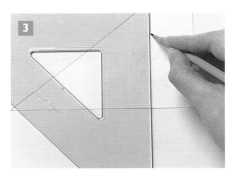

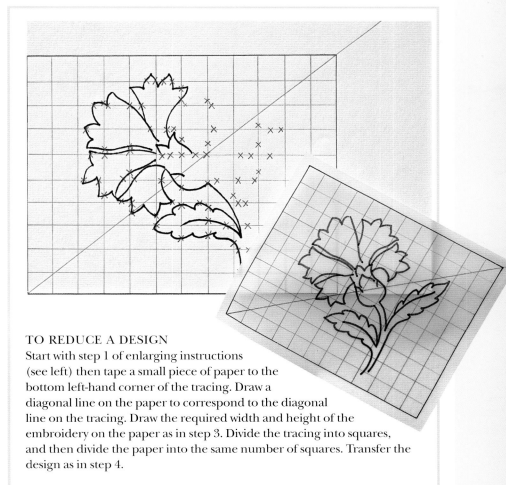

TO REDUCE A DESIGN

Start with step 1 of enlarging instructions (see left) then tape a small piece of paper to the bottom left-hand corner of the tracing. Draw a diagonal line on the paper to correspond to the diagonal line on the tracing. Draw the required width and height of the embroidery on the paper as in step 3. Divide the tracing into squares, and then divide the paper into the same number of squares. Transfer the design as in step 4.

| # Transferring a design

Once you have your pattern, you need to transfer it to your material. There are a number of methods for transferring an original design to fabric; some require specialist materials. If the item will be washed, it is a good idea to wash the material before you begin to prevent shrinkage later on. Then iron the fabric and, if necessary, cut it to size. Carefully position the design on the fabric before you transfer it by your chosen method.

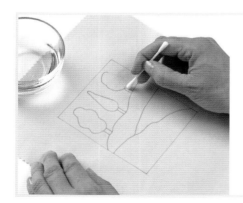

MAKING CORRECTIONS
Choose a water soluble pen if you want a line that will stay on the fabric until it is washed. If you use it on items that won't be washed, use a piece of damp cotton or a cotton bud to remove the lines

TRANSFERRING DESIGNS

DRAWING FREEHAND
Designs can be drawn directly onto the right side of fabric with a pencil or embroidery marker – a fine-tipped, water-soluble pen. Any lines that show afterward can be removed by dampening the fabric. With sheer fabrics such as organdy, muslin, or voile, draw the design on paper and go over the lines with a medium black felt-tip pen. When the ink is dry, place the fabric over the paper, and trace the design onto the fabric.

HOT-IRON TRANSFER
Copy your design onto tissue paper. Turn the paper over and trace the lines with an embroidery-transfer pencil. Pin the paper, transfer side down, to the fabric. Press down for a few seconds with an iron on low heat; moving the iron may cause smudges. Before unpinning, pull back a corner of the tissue paper to check that the transfer is visible on the fabric.

PRICK AND POUNCE
Trace the design onto tracing paper. Prick with a dressmaking pin along the design outlines. Pin the tracing to the right side of your material. Dot with an erasable marker through the pricked holes to mark an outline. Remove the tracing and join the dots with the marker. Dampen the fabric to wash away any visible pen lines.

TRACING WITH DRESSMAKER'S CARBON PAPER
Dressmaker's carbon paper is made especially for use on fabrics, and is nothing like stationery carbon paper. It works best on smooth fabrics. Use a light color on a dark fabric, and a dark color on a light fabric. Draw the design on thin paper. Place the carbon paper, ink side down, between the fabric and the design. Pin together at the corners, or hold down firmly with one hand. Trace over all the lines of the design with a sharp-pointed pencil or a tracing wheel, pressing down firmly. Check that you haven't missed any lines before finally unpinning.

PAPER TEMPLATES
This works well on any type of fabric, and is particularly useful for simple repeating motifs. Draw the design onto sturdy paper, and cut out each separate piece. Pin all the shapes in position on the fabric. Draw around them if the fabric is smooth or machine or hand baste around them if it is coarse. For a more durable template, draw your design onto flexible plastic.

Flat stitches

Of the four major groups of stitiches (flat, crossed, looped, and knotted), flat stitches are probably the simplest and easiest to learn. The stitches can be worked in varying sizes, grouped with other stitches in different combinations, or worked in different directions to form borders, outlines, and blocks of color in your designs.

EMBROIDERED POCKETS
Flat stitches used in combination can look very effective. Plain pockets make ideal surfaces on which to experiment with different stitches. Bands of encroaching satin stitch are set off by running stitch (see above left), while whipped running stitch is combined with half sun shapes worked in straight stitches (see above right).

SATIN STITCH
Work the straight stitches against each other to completely fill the area. Make sure the stitches are uniform.

ENCROACHING SATIN STITCH
Work the first row as for satin stitch. Work subsequent rows so that the head of the new stitch is between the bases of the stitches above.

SEED STITCH
Work very small uniform stitches to cover the area to be filled, changing stitch direction as desired. For a stronger effect, work two stitches close together instead.

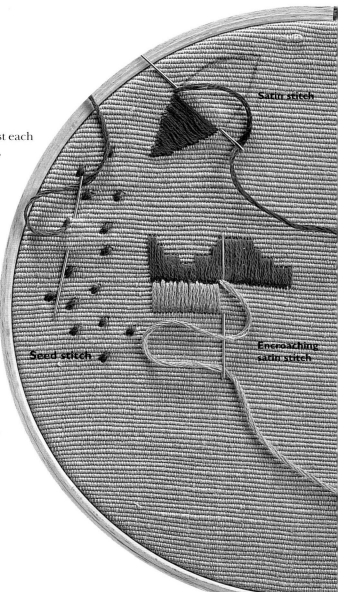

Satin stitch

Seed stitch

Encroaching satin stitch

FLAT STITCHES

RUNNING STITCH
Working from right to left, pass over 5 to 6 threads before inserting your needle into the fabric. Bring out your needle again, ready to make the next stitch, about 2 to 3 threads away.

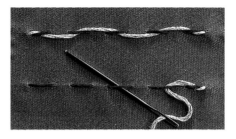

LACED RUNNING STITCH
Work a row of running stitches. Thread a round-pointed needle with contrasting thread and slide it between the stitches and the fabric alternately through the bottom of one stitch and then the top of the next stitch. Do not pick up any fabric.

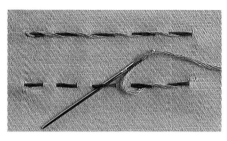

WHIPPED RUNNING STITCH
Work a row of running stitches. With a round-pointed needle, weave contrasting thread through each stitch from top to bottom, sliding the needle between the stitches and the fabric. Do not pick up any fabric.

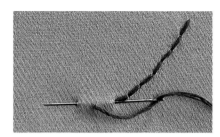

BACKSTITCH
Working from left to right, make a small stitch. Bring the needle to the right side again in front of the stitch just made. Make another backward stitch, inserting the needle at the point where the first stitch stops. Keep the length of the stitches even.

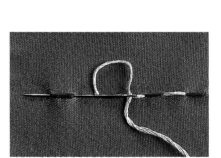

DOUBLE RUNNING STITCH
Work a row of running stitches. Work a second row in the same or a contrasting color, to fill the spaces between the stitches in the first row.

STEM STITCH
Work from left to right, making regular, slanted backstitches. The thread should always emerge slightly above the previous stitch.

SPLIT STITCH
Work in the same way as stem stitch, but the thread of the new stitch should split the thread of the previous stitch.

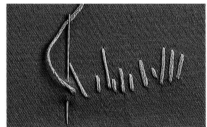

STRAIGHT STITCH
Single, spaced stitches may vary in size. Do not make them too long or too loose.

Crossed stitches

The most popular of all the embroidery
stitches, cross stitch is quick and easy to
master and can be used to create any
shape, image, and lettering. More
elaborate crossed stitches are
formed by stitches crossing
each other at differing angles. It's
simplest to work on a loosely woven
fabric such as canvas or Aida cloth; finer
fabrics can be used, although you
may have to baste lines on which
to work the stitches.

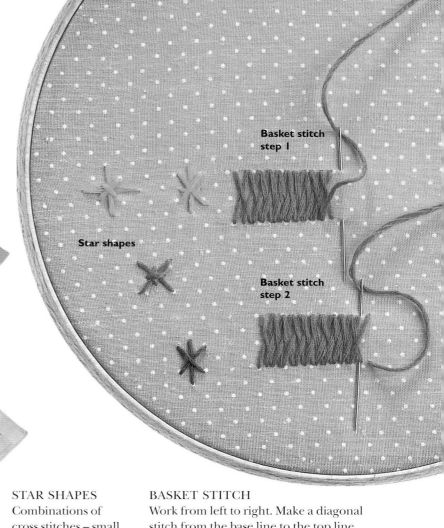

**Basket stitch
step 1**

Star shapes

**Basket stitch
step 2**

EMBROIDERED SQUARES
A few simple cross-stitch patterns can
transform plain or printed pieces of
material into handkerchiefs, coasters,
scarves, or mats.

STAR SHAPES
Combinations of
cross stitches – small,
over large, or
variations on the
same size – can be
used to create many
different star shapes.

BASKET STITCH
Work from left to right. Make a diagonal
stitch from the base line to the top line,
with the needle inserted vertically
downward through the design lines (1).
Make a vertical downward stitch to the left
and into the same holes as the two previous
crossed stitches (2).

CROSSED STITCHES

To work a neat row of crossed stitches, the head and base of each stitch should be the same number of rows apart.

BASIC CROSS STITCH

1 Work one or more evenly spaced diagonal stitches in one direction.

2 Cover with one or more diagonal stitches worked in the opposite direction.

LONG-ARMED CROSS STITCH

1 Bring the needle through at the stitch base line and make a long diagonal stitch to the right, at the desired height of the stitches. Measure the diagonal stitch, and bring out the needle half this distance to the left, on the top line.

2 Make a diagonal stitch to the base line; insert the needle directly below the point where the needle was inserted on the top line. Bring the needle out directly below the point where it emerged on the top line.

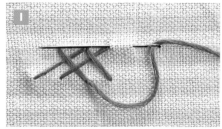

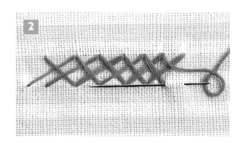

HERRINGBONE STITCH

Work from left to right. Bring the needle out on the base line, and insert it on the top line, a little to the right. Make a small stitch to the left along the top line. Then, insert the needle on the base line directly below the point where the needle first entered. The thread should be above the needle. Keep the spacing even.

TACKED HERRINGBONE STITCH

Work a row of herringbone stitch. In a contrasting colored thread, working from right to left, sew each cross together with a small vertical stitch.

CLOSED HERRINGBONE STITCH

Work in the same way as herringbone stitch but with no spaces left between the stitches. The diagonals should touch at the top and bottom.

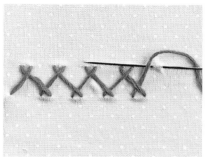

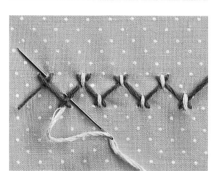

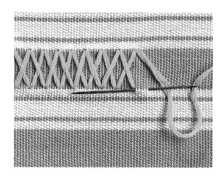

Looped stitches

All the stitches in this group are formed from loops that are held in place with small stitches. Looped stitches can be used both for outlining and for filling shapes. When used as filling stitches, they are generally worked in rows, and stitched in the same direction, to create an all-over texture. Chain stitch is the most important and versatile; it can be worked in thick yarns or fine silk threads.

EMBROIDERED COLLARS
Plain blouses and shirts often can be enlivened with imaginative stitch decoration. Lazy daisy and feather stitches are used on the collar and lapel shown here. Lazy daisies also are used to decorate the fabric buttons.

STRAIGHT OPEN CRETAN STITCH
Work by making short vertical stitches downward and upward alternately, with the thread always held down to the right under the tip of the needle.

FEATHER STITCH
Work vertically from top to bottom. Bring needle out at top center. Hold thread down with your left thumb, and insert needle to right and slightly below. Make a small slanting stitch toward the center, with the thread under the needle. Insert the needle again on the left side, and make a slanting stitch down toward the center, with the thread under the needle. Work looped stitches to left and right alternately.

DOUBLE FEATHER STITCH
Work the same way as feather stitch, but make two stitches instead of one.

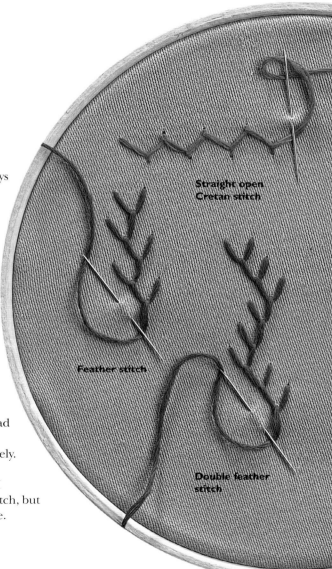

Straight open Cretan stitch

Feather stitch

Double feather stitch

LOOPED STITCHES

CHAIN STITCH

Bring the needle out to start the first stitch. Loop thread and hold it down with your left thumb. Insert the needle where it first emerged, and bring the tip out a short distance below this point. Keep the thread under the tip of the needle, and pull the needle through. For the next stitch, insert the needle into the hole from which it has just emerged.

LAZY DAISY STITCH (DETACHED CHAIN STITCH)

Work a single chain stitch, as described above. To secure the stitch, insert the needle just below the base of the loop and bring it out at the position for the next chain stitch.

BLANKET STITCH

Work from left to right. Bring the thread out at the position for the looped edging. Insert the needle above and a little to the left of this point as shown, and make a straight downward stitch, with the thread under the tip of the needle. Pull up the stitch to form the loop, and repeat.

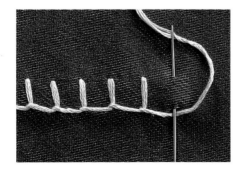

CHECKERED CHAIN STITCH

Thread the needle with two contrasting colored threads. Work as for chain stitch, keeping the thread not in use above the point of the needle.

OPEN CHAIN (LADDER) STITCH

Bring the needle out at the left side. Hold the thread down with the left thumb, and insert the needle to the right, at a point opposite where the thread emerged. Bring the needle out again at the left, with the thread under the needle. Continue anchoring the right side as for the left.

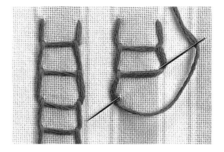

CLOSED CRETAN STITCH

1 Bring the needle through centrally at the left side of a shape. Make a stitch on the lower edge, with the needle pointing inward and the thread under the tip of the needle.

2 Make a stitch on the upper edge, with the needle pointing inward and the thread under the needle. Repeat steps 1 and 2 until the shape is filled.

Knotted stitches

These produce interesting surface textures and look particularly attractive when worked with a thick thread. Knotted stitches are formed by looping the thread around the needle, and then pulling the needle through the loops to form a knot or twist on the surface of the fabric.

EMBROIDERED CUFFS
Stitchery on blouse or shirt cuffs can be used to create an entirely individual look, which can be as subtle or as extrovert as you like. Toning or contrasting colors can be used according to your mood.

CORAL STITCH
Work from right to left. Bring the thread out, and hold it with your left thumb along the line to be worked. Make a small stitch under and over the looped working thread. Pull the thread through to form a knot. The spacing of the knots can be varied as required.

ZIG-ZAG CORAL STITCH
Bring the needle out at top left. Lay the thread across the fabric to right margin to form the first diagonal. Loop the thread; insert the needle and make a small diagonal stitch, bringing the needle tip out at the center of the loop. Pull the needle through the loop to form the knot. Lay the thread across the fabric to the left margin for the second diagonal, and repeat knot stitch. Continue knotting at right and left margins alternately to form a zig-zag.

PRACTICE MAKES PERFECT
If you haven't tried a particular knotted stitch before, work several samples on a piece of scrap fabric first because it takes a little practice to get the tension of the knots even. To prevent your thread getting tangled, always hold the loops of thread down with your left thumb when you pull the needle through.

KNOTTED STITCHES

FRENCH KNOT
Bring out the needle at the position for the knot. Twist the needle 2 or 3 times around the thread. Turn the needle and insert it just above where the thread first emerged. Holding the working thread taut with the left hand, pull the thread through to the back of the work. For a larger knot, use 2 or more strands of thread.

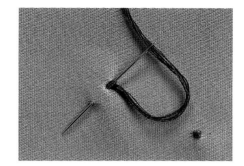

BULLION KNOT
Make a backstitch the size of desired knot. Bring the needle out half way from where it first emerged. Twist the thread around needle until of equal size to the backstitch. With left thumb on the coiled thread, pull the needle through. At insertion point, pull the needle and thread to the back, so the knot lies flat.

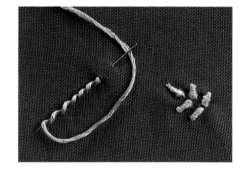

SCROLL STITCH
Bring the needle out. Loop the thread to the right. Insert the needle in the loop, and over the working thread as shown. Pull through to form a knot.

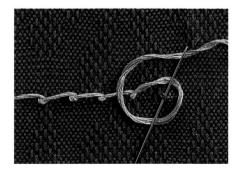

FOUR-LEGGED KNOT STITCH

1 Make a vertical stitch and bring the needle out at center right, ready to form horizontal leg of cross.

2 Slide the needle between the vertical stitch and the fabric, without picking up any fabric. Loop the thread around the needle, and pull the needle through to form the knot. Make a small horizontal stitch to the left, to form the last leg of the cross.

KNOTTED CHAIN (LINK) STITCH

1 Make an upward diagonal stitch, and bring out the needle directly below the point where it has just been inserted. Slide the needle between the stitch and the fabric, keeping the looped thread on the left.

2 Loop the working thread under the tip of the needle and pull through to form the knot.

BASKET LABELS

Embroidered labels are a fun way to turn inexpensive storage baskets and boxes into something special. Fixing with buttons makes them easy to attach to any material.

You will need

For each label:

• Iron-on interfacing

• Hessian or other closely woven cloth or canvas

• Embroidery floss in three contrasting colors such as blue, orange, and green. Use three strands when stitching.

• 4 buttons

MAKING UP

1 Press a 4½" (11 cm) square of iron-on interfacing to the center of a 10" (25 cm) square of canvas on the wrong side.

2 Enlarge the design, if necessary, to your chosen size and then copy it onto tracing paper. Using a water soluble marker and the Prick and Pounce method (see page 15), transfer it to the center of the square.

3 Fix the canvas in an embroidery hoop. Chain stitch (see page 21) the outline of the design.

4 Using two contrasting thread colors, backstitch (see page 17) the details.

5 Using the same color thread as used for the outline, work running stitch (see page 17) along the border of the design, stitching under and over three threads of the canvas.

6 Cut out the square, leaving 16 threads along each edge of the running stitch border. Fray the threads, leaving three threads unfrayed along each edge. Sew the label to the front of the basket with a button at each corner of the running stitch border.

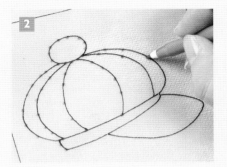

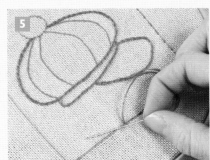

TEMPLATES

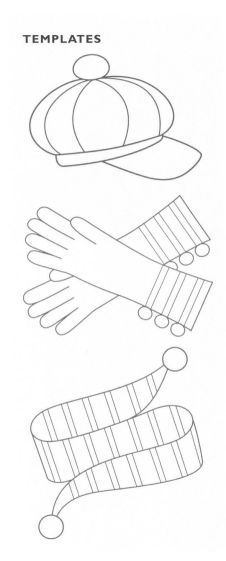

CROSS STITCH SERVING MAT

Create an eye-catching table mat on which to rest your cheese plate using our choice of cheese or charting out your own. The cross stitch lettering is easy to work as is the border in the same stitch.

You will need

- Graph paper, ruler, and pencil

- White sewing thread

- Sewing needle

- 19" × 13½" (48 × 34 cm) piece of cream colored 14-count Aida

- Basting thread

- Tapestry needle

- Stranded cotton embroidery floss

When working cross stitch lettering, you may find it easier to use a hoop. You will, however, have to remove your material and reposition it regularly.

MAKING UP

1 Referring to the alphabet on page 91, chart out the words Camembert, Mozzarella, Brie, and Feta onto a piece of graph paper. Leave one square's width space between each letter. Using a ruler, draw a horizontal line then a vertical line through the center of each word to find its center point.

2 Using white sewing thread, backstitch all around the edge of the fabric, ½" (1 cm) in from the edge. Using basting thread, mark a point at each corner 2½" (6 cm) in from the sides; this marks the outer corners of the design area.

3 Start with the word Camembert. Referring to the chart, count along the horizontal line to the center point. Take the fabric, with long sides at top and bottom, and count this number of blocks along from the top left basting mark; mark this position with line of vertical basting.

4 Referring to your chart, count along the vertical line to the center point of the word Camembert. Count this number of blocks down from the top left basting mark; mark this position with a line of horizontal basting. The point where the two lines of basting meet marks the center point of the word.

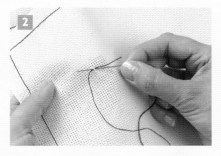
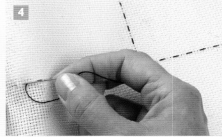
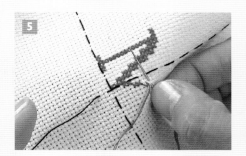
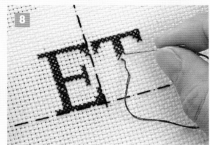

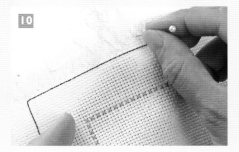

5 Thread the tapestry needle with two strands of embroidery floss, about 15" (38 cm) long. Starting at the center point and following your charted design, work the word Camembert in cross stitch (see page 19).

6 Turn the fabric through 180 degrees so that the word Camembert is in the bottom right corner (and upside down). Referring to the chart you made, repeat steps 3 and 4 to mark the center position of the word Mozzarella with lines of basting.

7 Stitch Mozzarella then turn the fabric through 90 degrees and, referring to the chart, repeat steps 3 and 4 to mark the center position of the word Feta.

8 Stitch Feta. Then turn the fabric through 180 degrees and, referring to the chart, repeat steps 3 and 4 to mark the center position of the word Brie. Stitch Brie. Remove all basting stitches.

9 If you like, make a cross stitch border about 1½" (4 cm) in from the outer edges to surround the lettering and another

cross stitch border in the center of the mat.

10 Using a pin, gently tease out the loose threads at the edges of the fabric up to the line of backstitching (see step 2) to to make a fringe. Press gently on the wrong side.

RECIPE BOOK COVER

Turn your recipe book into an heirloom by hand embroidering some strawberries and cupcakes with a scattering of flowers. Though designed for an 8½" × 11" (21.6 × 28.4 cm) book, it can be adjusted to suit any size book.

You will need

- 26½" × 18" (66 × 45 cm) piece washable woven check fabric

- Iron-on transfer pencil

- Six-stranded embroidery floss in sugar pink, yellow, primrose, violet, beige, white, and red

- Crewel needle

- Sewing thread to match fabric

TEMPLATES

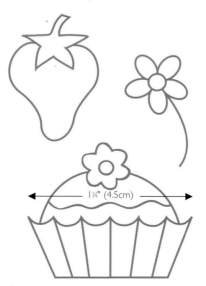

1¾" (4.5cm)

MAKING UP

1 Trace the motifs. On the reverse of the tracing, go over the lines using the transfer pencil, then position it on the fabric, to correspond with the center of the front cover. Transfer using a hot iron, according to the manufacturer's instructions.

2 Using a hoop and two strands of embroidery thread in your needle, embroider the flowers. Use stem stitch in green for the stems and satin stitch in yellow and violet for the centers and petals.

3 For the bases of the cup cakes, stitch rows of satin stitch between the marked lines, altering the direction of each row of stitches. For large areas, such as the strawberries, stitch using long-and-short satin stitch.

4 When all the motifs have been stitched, add little stars in yellow thread by making five straight stitches radiating from a single point. Scatter French knots in several colors, over the background.

5 Press the work carefully on the reverse, placing a folded towel underneath to prevent the embroidery from becoming flattened. Press under 1¼" (3 cm) all around and hand- or

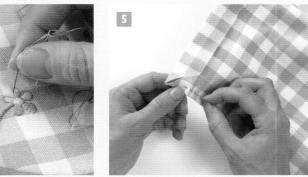

machine stitch ¼" (5 mm) from the folded edges. Fold under a further 1½" (4 cm) on the two long edges, then fold in 3¼" (8 cm) at both sides.

6 Slipstitch the corners to create two narrow pockets for the covers of the book to slip inside. Trim any loose threads.

TIP
Using washable fabric means the book cover can easily be removed and hand laundered should it become stained.

| # Monograms and lettering

Embroidered pieces are often personalized with monograms, initials, names, and messages. Cross stitch (see page 18), for example, has been used traditionally to work the name and date on samplers, and is still the most popular lettering stitch for embroidered pictures. Satin stitch creates lettering that stands proud of the fabric. Ribbon and braid also can be used, and often imparts greater variety to a piece of work. Alphabets, such as the ones on pages 90-91, can be traced and transferred to your background fabric.

LETTER SPACING

The spacing of letters is crucial to getting a good effect. Before you start stitching, trace the letters, numbers, or words onto paper then hold the paper away from you and study the effect. If necessary, adjust the spacing before transferring the lettering to the fabric.

BRAID AND RIBBON LETTERING

For joined lettering, try to plan out the design so that only one piece of ribbon or braid is required for the complete design. If you must add a separate piece, place it underneath the ribbon or braid previously laid down. Raised braids can be couched (see page 35) in a matching or contrasting color.

1 Fine ribbon and braid can be used for lettering. Hem the short ends by pressing the narrow raw edges to the wrong side. Stitch in place down the center with small running or back stitches (see page 17).

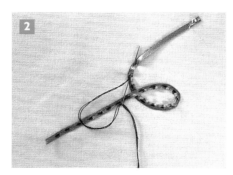

2 When you reach an intersection, leave a gap in the running stitches. On the return, thread the ribbon or braid through this gap, and continue stitching.

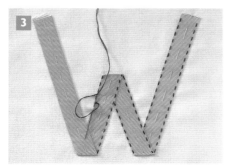

3 A wide braid or double-sided ribbon may be twisted over to form angles and corners for straight-sided lettering. Baste in position and press. Then stitch along both edges so that they lie flat and even.

STITCHED LETTERS

Satin stitch (see page 16) and its variations (see below), are ideal for working initials. Before you embark on a monogram, practice working the shapes to obtain a smooth outline.

NEGATIVE SATIN STITCH

This is an effective technique for monograms and crests. Choose a simple, well defined letter shape. Work the background in satin stitch, leaving the letters in unstitched fabric. Outline the design in stem stitch (see page 17) or chain stitch (see page 21).

PADDED SATIN STITCH

Raising the satin stitch above the surface of the fabric gives it more definition. Fill in the outlined area with satin stitch. Then, working in a different direction, add a second layer of satin stitch.

MONOGRAMMED POCKET

Any plain garment — a blouse, nightshirt, or dress — is the perfect setting for a decorative, embossed monogram. Using couched ribbons produces a raised design, which is very attractive. Make it on a plain scrap of fabric, which you can then hem and use to create a pocket, or trim it to fit over an existing pocket.

Any design incorporating lettering should be easy to read. You can trace the alphabet on page 90 or use examples in books and magazines. If possible, place your fabric in a hoop once the letters are transferred, so that you can keep the stitches even and prevent the fabric from puckering.

Narrow silk ribbon is the best choice for this design as it is soft and flexible and can be coaxed into neat folds with the tip of your needle.

You will need

• ¼" (5 mm) silk ribbon

• Matching sewing thread

• Fabric remnant

• Crewel embroidery needle

MAKING THE POCKET

1 Carefully trace your chosen letters, ensuring that the spacing between them is pleasing to the eye. On the reverse of the tracing, go over the lines using an iron-on transfer pencil.

2 Use a hot iron to transfer the motif to a piece of cotton fabric. This fabric should be at least ¾" (2 cm) bigger all around than the pocket on your nightshirt or other garment, and in any case large enough to fit in a small embroidery hoop that will accommodate the entire monogram.

3 Thread a large embroidery needle with a length of silk ribbon. Bring the needle out at one edge of the first letter to be embellished, leaving a small end on the wrong side of the work. Push the needle into the fabric at another point on the letter and pull the ribbon through; do not pull too tightly.

4 Thread a finer needle with sewing thread to match the ribbon. Hold the ribbon in place over one portion of the letter while you slipstitch the edges to the fabric, using tiny stitches. When you come to a curve, you may need to make a fold in the ribbon to accommodate the change in direction. If necessary, adjust

the length of ribbon by pulling a little more through from the back. If the center of the ribbon is too prominent, stitch it down with a few stitches, creating attractive pleats and folds.

5 As you come to the end of one portion of the letter, bring another length of ribbon to the front. At times, you will need to cut off the ribbon and start again at another place on the motif.

6 Make sure you stitch the cut ends neatly to the fabric on the reverse of the design, so that they don't show through at the front of the work.

7 Trim the fabric to the size of the existing pocket, or to create a pocket if there is none. Allow turnings of between ¼" (5 mm) and ½" (1 cm) all around, and twice this amount at the top if you need to make a double hem for the pocket opening.

8 Turn under seam allowances and press, pin, and baste, then slipstitch to the nightshirt. You may want to add topstitching so that it is really secure.

OPTIONS

Fine silk ribbon is available in a wide range of colors. Here, a variegated ribbon was used for extra interest.

This technique is a quick and easy method of both outlining a design and filling large shapes rapidly to produce solid areas of color. At its simplest, one strand of thread is laid on the fabric and stitched down at intervals with another strand. More than one strand can be laid down at a time to create bold outlines. Textured and metallic threads, which won't pass through the fabric easily, can be laid down with finer thread.

LAIDWORK

This is a continuation of couching. Long threads are laid vertically and horizontally on the fabric to form a grid pattern, and then secured at the intersections with small, slanting stitches using a separate (often differently colored) thread. Further embroidery stitches can then be worked in the framework over a number of squares. For the best results, use an embroidery frame in order to keep the fabric taut, and make sure that the grid threads are evenly spaced.

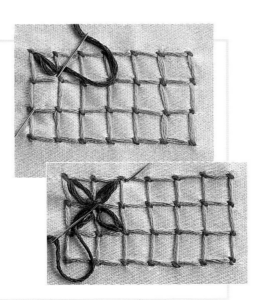

Gold and silver threads, which are naturally more expensive than cotton or silk, are couched because all of the precious metal remains on the surface.

COUCHING TECHNIQUES

BASIC COUCHING

Work from right to left. Bring out the strand(s) to be laid and use your left thumb to hold in place. Bring out the couching thread just below the laid strand(s). Make a vertical stitch over the laid strands, bringing the needle out to the left, below the laid strands, ready for the next stitch. At the end of the line, take both the couching and laid threads through to the back of the work, and secure.

TO FILL AN AREA

1 Work a line of basic couching. At the end of the line, turn the loose laid thread to the right and make a horizontal stitch across the turning point.

2 Turn the work upside-down and couch a second row of threads next to the first, placing the stitches between those on the previous row. Continue until the area is filled.

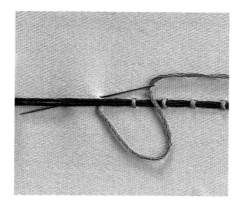

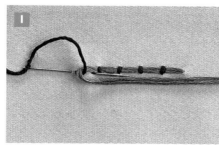

TO COUCH A CIRCLE

1 Bring out the needle with the couching thread at the center of the circle, and pass the needle through the looped laid thread. Re-insert the needle at the center to secure the laid thread.

2 With your left thumb, guide the laid thread into a spiral. Bring needle out a short distance away and couch over it.

3 Make sure all couching stitches line up as shown, as if on the spokes of a wheel. When finished, bring the threads to the back and secure.

VARIATION
Couching can be worked with two contrasting colored threads, and with open chain stitch (see page 21).

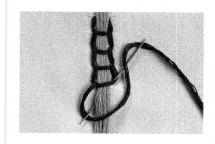

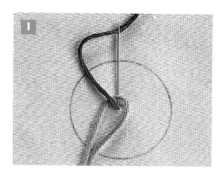

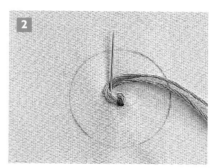

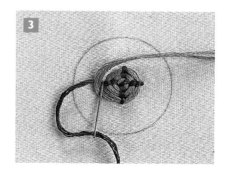

BOTTLE BAG

Make that gift of champagne or wine even more festive by creating a carrier bag with a couched design of vine leaves and grapes. The lining should help keep the contents cool, if necessary. Knotted leather ties make it easy to carry.

You will need

- ½ yard (45 cm) medium-weight fabric

- Remnant lightweight buckram

- Embroidery floss in green, violet, and purple

- 1 yard (90 cm) leather cord

TEMPLATE

MAKING THE BAG

Cut two rectangles of fabric and one rectangle of lightweight buckram, each 18" × 15" (45 × 38 cm) for the bag and lining. Cut two rectangles of fabric and one rectangle of lightweight buckram, each 6¼" × 4¼" (15.5 × 10.5 cm), for the base.

1 Mark the center of one fabric piece with a row of pins parallel with the short edges. Enlarge the design, as necessary, and transfer it (see page 15) to the fabric, matching the upper edges to the row of pins. Fix the material in an embroidery hoop. Couch the leaf and stalks (see page 35) in green, using 1 strand over 6 strands. To couch the thick stem, place rows of 6 threads side by side and stagger the holding stitches made with a single thread.

2 Using 3 green strands, backstitch the tendril.

3 To couch the grapes and retain their shape, bring 6 purple strands to the right side at the outside edge of each grape. Lay the strands along the circumference of the grape and stitch over them with 1 strand at ⅛" (3 mm) intervals. Continue to the center of the grape. Insert the 6 strands into the wrong side at the center and fasten off.

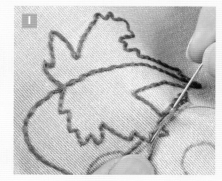

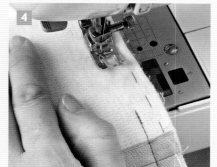

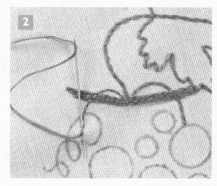

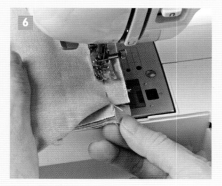

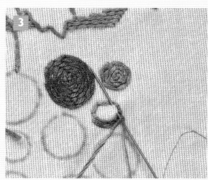

Couch the large grapes with purple and the small grapes with violet.

4 Make up the bag: Baste the larger piece of buckram between the fabric pieces with the right sides facing outward. Stitch the short edges of the fabric pieces together (right sides facing) taking a ⅝" (1.5 cm) seam allowance, forming a tube. Finish ⅝" (1.5 cm) above the lower edge. Press the seams open; neaten with a zig-zag stitch.

5 Hand sew a 1½" (3.5 cm) hem at the upper edge.

6 Baste the buckram base between the fabric bases with the right sides facing outward. Baste the base to the lower edge of the bag, matching the seam to one corner. Snip the lower edge of the bag at the other corners to pivot the seam. Stitch the base to the bag. Snip the seam allowance across the corners. Neaten the raw edges with zig-zag stitch. Turn right side out. Press the bag from the corners of the base.

7 Make two small holes – one in each side of the bag, and blanket stitch (see page 21) around the circumference. Thread through the leather cord.

| VELVET SCARF

Couching adds richness to a fabric and enables you to experiment with different design motifs. Here, simple flowers in a shade that echoes the satin backing are scattered over the toning raised grid to add textural interest to a shimmering velvet scarf.

You will need

- 1½ yards (135 cm) panne velvet, 12" (30 cm) wide

- 1½ yards (135 cm) satin, 12" (30 cm) wide

- Silk embroidery floss in 3 different colors

- Embroidery needle

- Basting thread

- Matching sewing thread

- Knitting needle, if necessary

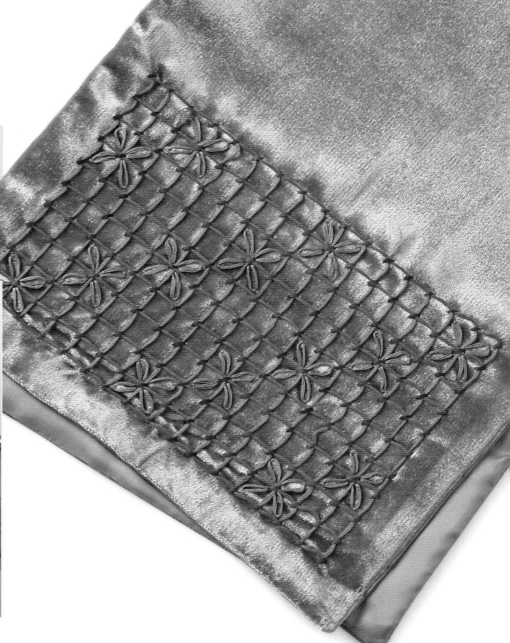

MAKING THE SCARF

1 Take your length of velvet and decide on how deep you want the panel of embroidery at each end; use basting or pins to mark the areas and make sure you leave allowances of 1" (2.5 cm) around the raw edges.

2 Using 6 strands of color A, work the horizontal and vertical stiches of an open lattice pattern across the marked area (see page 35) at one end of the velvet. Change to color B and, using 6 strands, work the couching stitches that secure the lattice in place.

3 Change to color C and using 4 strands, work a series of detached chain stitches across the lattice work to make a flower pattern. You can position these at regular intervals or create a more random design as wished.

4 Repeat steps 2 and 3 at the other end of the velvet. Remove any basting stitches. Put the velvet and satin right sides together, matching raw edges. Pin and then baste all around.

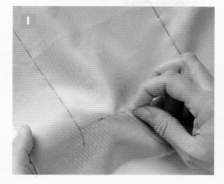

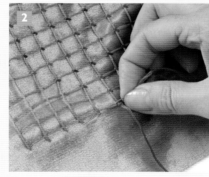
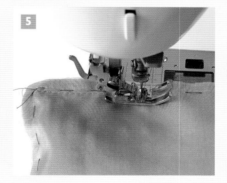
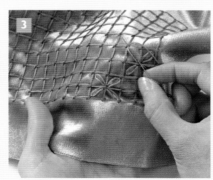
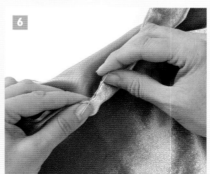

5 Machine stitch around the edges, leaving an 8" (20 cm) gap at the center of one long side. Make sure you don't stitch over your embroidery. Snip across the allowance at the corners to reduce the bulk of the fabric. Turn the scarf to the right side through the gap. Use a knitting needle to gently push the fabric into the corners, if necessary.

6 If the care instructions for your fabric allow, press lightly along the seams, covering your embroidery work with a cloth before you begin, and turning under the allowances at the gap. If your fabrics cannot be ironed, then lightly crease the seams between your fingertips. Slipstitch the gap closed to finish.

TIP
When working with very slippery fabrics such as satin, silk, and silk velvets, it is a good idea to place a sheet of tissue paper between the layers to keep them from sliding away from each other. Stitch through all the layers and pull the tissue away afterward.

Drawn threadwork

A popular way to create decorative fabric is to remove some of the warp and weft threads of coarse open-weave material and to pull together with embroidery floss the remaining threads in clusters to form open patterns. The floss should be similar in thickness to a single thread of the ground fabric, and used with a round-pointed tapestry needle.

MITERED CORNERS

1 Press raw edges to the wrong side of the fabric. Turn under the folded edge again by the same amount to form a double hem, and press. Open fabric.

2 Crease marks will form 4 squares at each corner. Taking 1 corner at a time, cut it off by cutting inner square in half diagonally. Fold in sides so that edges just meet at inner corner of inner square. Turn under raw edges; press.

3 Refold edges and pin and baste hems. By hand, slipstitch mitered corner edges then machine or hand stitch hem.

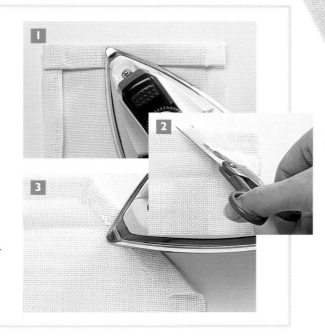

For the most sophisticated effects, use embroidery floss or yarns that tone in with the background fabric.

DRAWN THREADWORK TECHNIQUES

HOW TO REMOVE THE FABRIC THREADS

1 Cut your chosen fabric to size, allowing for a mitered hem around all 4 sides (see page 40). Mark out the hem allowance with a row of basting stitches. Decide on the number of threads that will make up the depth of the border and mark the inner border line, then mark the center point on each side.

2 Using a pair of sharp embroidery scissors, carefully cut the horizontal fabric threads at the center mark on each side of the border. Gently ease out the threads with a tapestry needle until you reach the corners.

3 Trim loose thread ends. Then fold them back, and backstitch over the ends. Remove the basting stitches. Turn up hem allowance, and baste in position, ready for hem stitching.

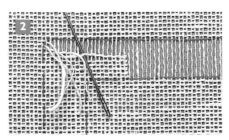

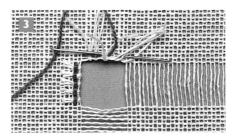

HEM STITCH

1 Work from left to right on the wrong side of the fabric. Bring needle out two threads below hem, and opposite first loose thread in border. Make a diagonal stitch to the right, and insert the needle under the first 3 or more loose threads in the border; pull together.

2 Make a vertical stitch, bringing the needle out on the wrong side, to the right of tbe bundle and 2 threads below the hem. Repeat.

LADDER STITCH VARIATION
Complete a row of hem stitch. Turn the work upside-down and work hem stitch along the opposite edge of the border, catching the same loose threads into bundles, forming a ladder-like pattern.

TO FINISH CORNERS
If the open squares at the corners are small, they can be left as they are, or they can be reinforced with blanket stitch (see page 21).

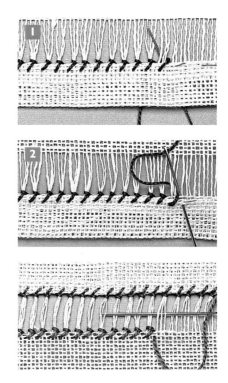

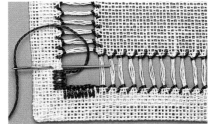

Lacy patterns can be produced by pulling tightly on looping stitches wrapped around fabric threads. You need an even-weave fabric and strong thread of a similar weight to a single thread of your fabric. Use a round-pointed needle to exaggerate the holes, but make sure it will still slip between the threads easily.

Miter the edges (see page 40) if you're making place mats or napkins so they lie flat; pin stitching (see box) creates a decorative finish.

Run a line of basting stitches in a contrasting color across the length and width of your fabric to help you count the stitches, and remove them when the work is finished. Work the stitch patterns in rows, starting at the center and moving outward. Count the fabric threads carefully, and always pull the embroidery thread tight; a frame can make stitching easier.

Secure the first thread with a few backstitches on the wrong side of the work. Then, when you have finished a row of the pattern, unpick the stitches, and weave the loose thread under some of the embroidery stitches. Secure all other threads by weaving the ends under worked stitches.

PIN-STITCHED HEM

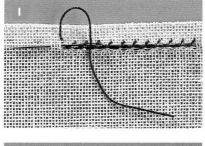

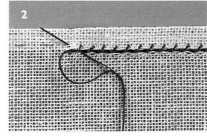

1 Bring needle out on right side, 2 threads above folded hem. Insert needle 2 threads down (through single thickness) just under hem and bring it out 4 threads to the left. Backstitch over same 4 threads and pull tight.

2 Make a second backstitch over the 4 threads, and bring out needle 2 stitches above hemline to start next stitch sequence.

COIL FILLING STITCH

1 Bring out needle on right side. Make 2 vertical satin stitches across 4 threads, into same holes. Make a third satin stitch into the top hole, bringing out the needle 4 threads to the left, on the base line of the stitches just worked.

2 To begin next row, bring out needle 4 threads below and 2 threads to the right of the stitches just made. Continue working rows from right to left, and left to right, alternately.

HONEYCOMB STITCH

1 Bring the needle out on right side. Insert needle 3 threads to the right, and bring it out 3 threads down. Backstitch into the base of stitch just made, and bring it out 3 threads down. Insert the needle 3 threads to the left, and bring it out 3 threads down. Backstitch into the base of stitch just made, and bring it out 3 threads down. Repeat to end of row.

2 Turn the work at the end of the row, and embroider the next row in the same way.

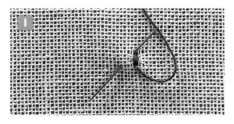

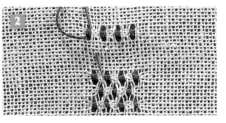

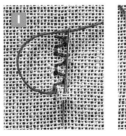
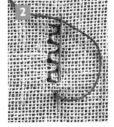

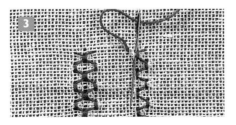

FAGGOT STITCH

1 Bring out the needle on the right side of the fabric. Work diagonally, and make horizontal and then vertical stitches over an equal number of threads alternately.

2 On the next row, make squares by working into the holes of the previous row.

CHESSBOARD FILLING STITCH

1 Work 3 rows of satin stitch from left to right, and right to left, alternately. Each satin stitch is worked over 3 threads, and each block is made up of 3 rows of 8 stitches.

2 At end of the third row, turn the work as shown, and bring out the needle 3 vertical threads down and one horizontal thread to the left, ready to start the next block.

3 Repeat step 1. Work all other blocks in the same way, turning the work after each to change the stitch direction.

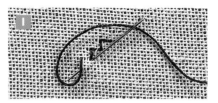

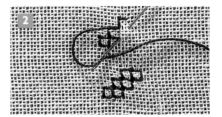

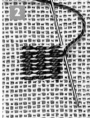

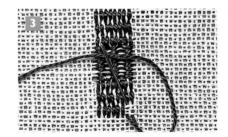

Simple wooden serving pieces decorated with embroidered cloths in openwork are a feature of Scandinavian design. Adapt this mat to dress up any plain tray or tabletop.

You will need

- Evenweave fabric (28-count linen was used here)

- Basting thread

- Embroidery scissors

- Tapestry needle, size 24

- One skein stranded cotton embroidery floss

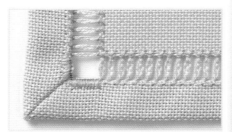

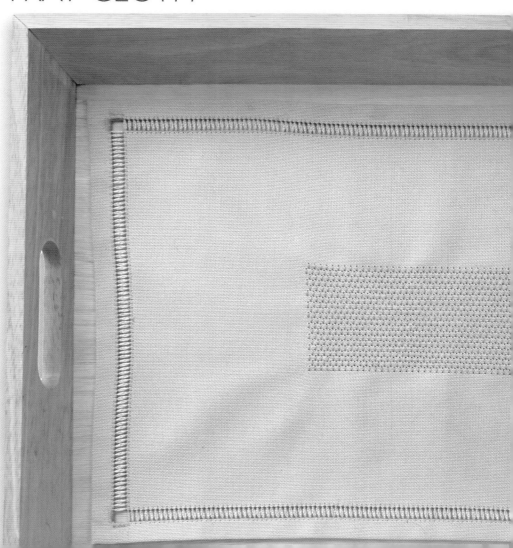

Top: A close-up view of coil filling stitch, which appears in the center of the cloth.
Bottom: A close-up view of one of the mitered corners showing the loose ends secured with blanket stitch and the open chain border.

MAKING THE CLOTH

1 Measure the length and width inside your tray to get the finished size of the cloth. Add 2" (5 cm) to both the length and width to get the size you will need; cut your fabric to these measurements

2 Turn under ½" (1 cm) all around and press. Turn under the same amount and press again. Pin and baste the first line close to the turned edge; this marks the outer edge of the drawn threadwork border (see page 41).

3 Count in 8 threads from this line of basting to find the inner edge of the border; mark this with basting. Mark the center point of each side of the border with basting. Carefully cut the horizontal fabric threads at the center mark on each side of the border.

4 Ease out the threads between your basting guidelines with a tapestry needle until you reach the corners.

5 Trim the loose thread ends and secure to the wrong side with backstitch. Turn up the double hem as before, mitering the corners (see page 40). Press and stitch the miters in place. Baste all around the hem.

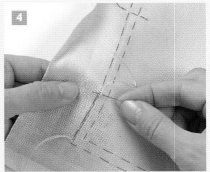

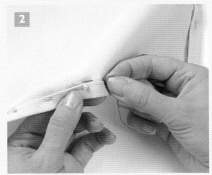

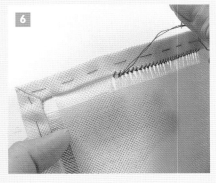

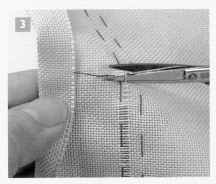

6 Using 2 strands of embroidery floss and a tapestry needle, work open chain (ladder) stitch all around the border (see pages 21 and 41), stitching the hem as you go, and finish the corners with blanket stitch (see page 21). Finish off the loose ends and press on the wrong side.

7 Fold the fabric in half widthwise and lengthwise to find the center point; mark this with small basting stitches. Measure from this point to the inner edge of the border on one short side. Find the center point between the two and mark with a pin. Repeat on the opposite side. Measure from the center point to the inner edge of the border on one long side. Find the center point between the two and mark with a pin. Repeat on the opposite side.

8 Using basting thread, mark out a rectangle in the center of the fabric along the lines marked by the pins. This marks the central pulled-threadwork rectangle. Work coil filling stitch to fill this rectangle (see page 43). Remove all basting, finish off loose ends and press on the wrong side.

CUTWORK CUSHION

Another form of openwork embroidery, cutwork entails removing some of the top fabric to enable a decorative underlayer to show through. Stitching the cutwork edges with close blanket stitch in contrasting colors adds to the decorative look of the cushion.

You will need

- Square cushion pad, 13½" (35 cm)

- 1 yard (90 cm) mediumweight fabric

- 15" (37.5 cm) square of satin or other shiny material in a contrasting color

- Erasable marker

- Stranded embroidery cotton in four different colors

- Sharp embroidery scissors

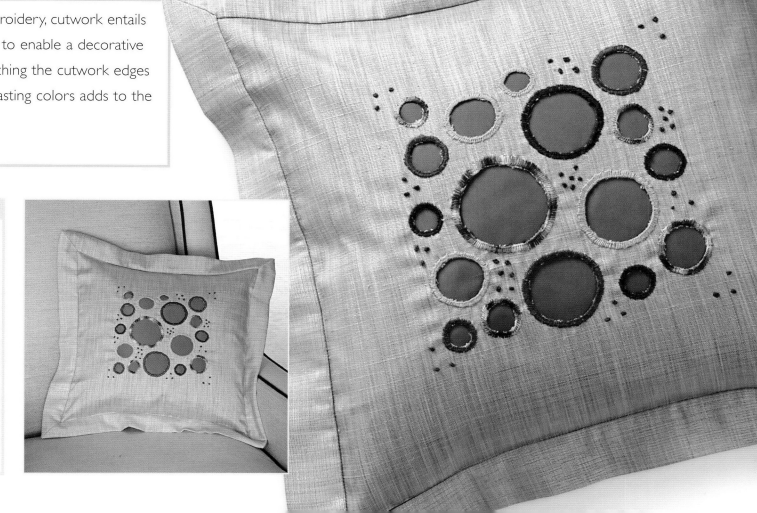

MAKING UP

From the mediumweight fabric, cut a 15" (37.5 cm) square for the front, a 15" × 22" (37.5 × 55 cm) rectangle for the back, and four 4½" × 18" (11 × 45 cm) rectangles for the borders. Cut the back piece in half.

1 Create differently sized circle templates and arrange them randomly across the front. When you're happy with the spacing, pin each in place. Use an erasable marker and draw around each one; remove the paper circles.

2 Using 2 strands of embroidery floss, make small running stitches around the outside of each circle and with another color, make another circle about ¼" (5 mm) to ⅜" (8 mm) away, depending on the size of the circle.

3 Work close blanket stitch (see page 21) between the two lines.

4 On the back side, carefully cut out the inside of the circle close to the base of the stitches. Pin the satin to the back and using 6 strands of floss, work French knots (see page 23) around the circles.

5 Make a double ½" (1 cm) hem on the center edge of each back piece. Pin the pieces to the front, with right sides

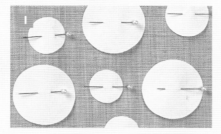

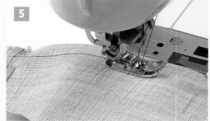

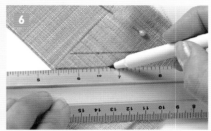

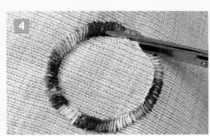

facing out. Match the raw edges and overlap the hemmed edges; pin and stitch ½" (1 cm) all around.

6 Fold each border in half, right sides facing. Overlap the ends of two borders at right angles with the fold edges on the outer sides and the ends projecting by ⅝" (1.5 cm); pin. Draw a seam line diagonally across the corner between the points where the borders intersect. Mark the allowance ½" (1 cm) outside the seam line. Turn the border over and repeat. Trim along outer lines. Repeat with other two borders.

7 Unpin the borders and open out. Mark the seamline on the unmarked part. Place the two borders together, right sides facing, and stitch along the marked lines starting and finishing ⅝" (1.5 cm) in.

8 Trim the point, press seam open and stitch all four corners similarly. Pin the right side of one border edge to the right side of the front, making sure all corners fit. Separately stitch each edge, ending and starting ⅝" (1.5 cm) in.

9 Press the seam allowance to the right side along the remaining border edge. Place it over the back of the cushion so that it just covers the previous stitching and seam is enclosed. Slipstitch in place.

This is an attractive way to shape and decorate clothes, and all sorts of items for the home such as cushions, lampshades, and curtains. You have to smock the fabric before making it up into a garment or other item. The amount of fabric needed is usually three times the finished width of the smocked area.

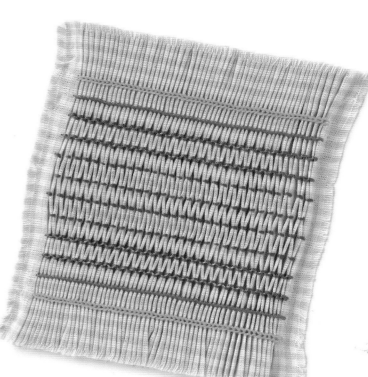

It's always a good idea to make a sample of smocking stitches to see how they affect the fabric. From the top down, the sample shows wheat stitch, stem stitch, cable stitch, and honeycomb stitch.

GATHERING THE FABRIC

Use iron-on smocking dot transfers, placed in line with your fabric's threads, as stitch guidelines. Work the gathering stitch rows from right to left, on the fabric's wrong side using a crewel needle and contrasting strong cotton thread; the latter makes removing the gathering thread easier when finished.

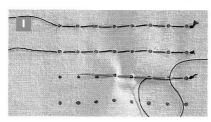

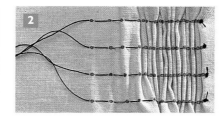

1 Cut a length of thread, longer than the row of dots to be gathered, and tie a knot in the end. Make running stitches along each row, picking up a piece of the fabric at each dot. Leave thread ends loose.

2 Pull up each gathering thread to the required width and tie together in pairs at the end of the rows. Make sure all pleats are even and that the gathers are not pulled too tightly.

Any supple fabric can be smocked. Regular repeating patterns, such as checks and dots, are popular because the pattern can be used as a guideline for the gathering stitches. Stitches are worked on the right side of the gathered fabric from left to right, beginning at the top left-hand corner. Make sure the embroidery thread is attached and fastened off very securely. Hold the needle parallel to the gathering threads, and take the stitches through about one-third of the depth of each pleat, to keep them elastic, and to ensure that the embroidery thread doesn't become entangled with the gathering thread. Leave the first row of gathers free of embroidery so that the smocked panel can be joined to another piece. Smocking stitches vary considerably in tension, so work a sample first to see how tight or loose a stitch will be. Intricate patterns can be made with a combination of stitches, although equally impressive results can be achieved by working only one or two.

SMOCKING STITCHES

STEM STITCH

Use this stitch for the top row of smocking. Bring the needle out to the left of the first fold. Make a stitch through the top of each fold, keeping the thread below the needle.

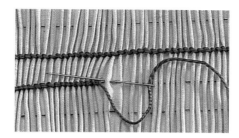

CABLE STITCH

1 Bring the needle out to the left of the first fold. With the thread below the needle, make a stitch over the second fold, and bring the needle out between the first and second folds.

2 With the thread above the needle, make a stitch over the third fold, and bring the needle out between the second and third folds. Continue to the end of the row, keeping the thread above, then below, the needle.

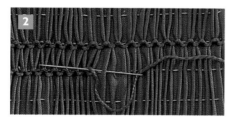

WHEAT STITCH

Work a row of stem stitch, then work a second row just below, keeping the thread above the needle to alter the stitch direction.

HONEYCOMB STITCH

1 This stitch is worked across two lines of gathering stitches. Bring the needle out at the left of the first fold on top of the line of gathering stitches. Backstitch over the first two folds to draw them together. Make a second backstitch over the two folds, bringing the needle out at the lower line of the gathering stitches, between the first and second fold.

2 Backstitch over the second and third folds to draw them together. Make a second backstitch over these folds, bringing the needle out at the top line of gathering stitches, between the second and third fold.

3 Continue working stitches on the top and bottom lines of gathering stitches alternately.

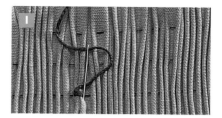

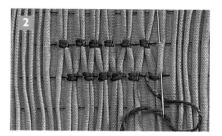

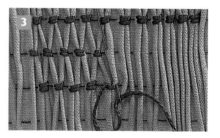

TO FINISH

When a smocked piece is finished, steam press on the wrong side, or lay a damp cloth on top and lightly pass a hot iron over the work, taking care not to flatten it. Then remove the gathering threads.

If you find that the smocking is too tight, take out the gathering stitches, lay the work wrong side on the ironing board, and pin it out to size. Steam press as above.

SMOCKED BANGLE BAG

Create an eye-catching bag that's great for special occasions – particularly if the silk fabric tones in with your outfit. The bamboo handles are just big enough to slip over a wrist.

You will need

- Silk fabric 32" × 12½" (80 × 31 cm)

- Dressmaker's pencil, card, and ruler for marking up the fabric

- Basting thread

- Embroidery floss

- Two 4" (10 cm) diameter bamboo rings

MAKING THE BAG

1 Turn under each long edge of the fabric by ¼" (5 mm); press. Turn under each edge again by ½" (1 cm); press and pin. Machine- or handstitch each hem in place.

2 Lay out the fabric flat so that the short edges are at the top and bottom. Mark your first row of dots 5" (12.5 cm) down from the top edge. Position the first and last dots in the row ½" (1 cm) from the turned edge and make the dots ⅜" (8 mm) apart. Make five more identical rows below the first one so that the rows are ½" (1 cm) apart. Turn the fabric through 180 degrees and repeat the process.

3 Gather up the fabric in both panels as described on page 48. Then use two strands of embroidery floss to work smocking stitch across the panels. Here, each panel is made up of five rows of honeycomb stitch (see page 49) but you could use a different stitch if preferred.

4 Finish off and press the smocked fabric (see page 49). Fold the fabric in half widthwise, right sides together and matching up the panels of smocking; press lightly along the fold. Pin the sides together as far as the smocking panels and then slipstitch the seams together.

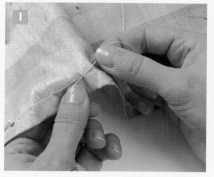

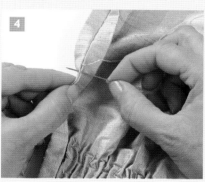

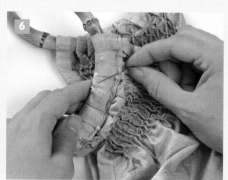

5 Lay the bag out flat and place one of the bangles at the top, so the edge of the bangle is just above the top edge of the smocking. Fold the fabric over the bangle so that the bangle is enclosed and pin in place – you will have to gather up the fabric to fit. Trim the excess fabric to within ⅝" (1.5 cm) of the pins. Remove the pins and bangle and trim the other side of the bag to match.

6 Turn under each top edge of the bag by ⅝" (1.5 cm); press and stitch in place. Then turn one top edge over one bangle and baste to secure, gathering up the fabric as you go to fit. Handstitch the turning in place. Repeat to attach the other bangle to the other side. Turn the bag to the right side.

FINISHING TOUCH

Why not jazz up this bag with two beaded tassels? Simply insert at the corners before you stitch up the sides in step 4.

SMOCKED TUBE TOP

This summery top, held together by silk ribbon ties at the back and shoulders, is made from a length of patterned cotton lawn smocked to size. It's important to test your smocking skills before embarking on this project. Using some spare fabric, work your chosen stitches to see how tightly the fabric is pulled and then adjust the fabric size before cutting.

You will need

- Fabric

- Dressmaker's pencil, card, and ruler for marking up the fabric

- Tissue paper

- Basting thread

- Embroidery floss

- Silk ribbon

Certain smocking stitches such as wheat and stem stitch will hold the fabric in place, while others, such as honeycomb, are more elastic. Bear this in mind if choosing other stitches to use on the top.

MAKING THE TOP

Measure around your chest below the bust. Multiply this measurement by 3 (or more if your smocking holds the fabric tightly) and add 2½"(6 cm) for turnings; this is measurement A. Decide on how long you want the cropped top to be and add 2½" (6 cm)for turnings; this is measurement B.

1 Cut a piece of fabric A × B. Turn under each long edge ⅝"(1.5 cm), then turn under each one again the same amount to make a double hem; press. Machine- or hand-stitch each hem. Turn under double hems on the short edges in the same way and stitch in place.

2 Mark up the fabric for gathering, as described on page 48 (using tracing paper, if necessary[see box]), making a panel of dots at the top of the fabric and one at the bottom – the fabric between the two panels is unsmocked. Make the dots ¼"(5 mm) apart and the rows ⅜"(8 mm) apart. Make the top row of dots on the top panel line up just below the hem stitching, and have the bottom row of dots on the bottom panel line up just above the hem stitching. Have the outermost rows of dots on both panels line up inside the hem stitching of the side edges.

TIP

On a finely patterned fabric, you can draw the dots onto tracing paper and sew through it, tearing off the paper when you've finished.

3 Gather up the fabric in both panels as described on page 48. Then use 2 strands of embroidery floss to work the smocking across the panels. Here, there is a row of wheat stitch followed by one of stem stitch then 4 rows of honeycomb stitch (see page 49) – this is reversed for the bottom panel. You can chose other stitches if you prefer.

4 Finish off, securing all loose ends at the back, and press the smocked fabric (see page 49). Cut six 10" (25 cm) lengths of ribbon for the ties. Pin one length at the top and bottom of each short side, turning under the end of each tie. Pin the remaining ties to the center of each short side in the same way. Stitch each tie securely in place.

5 Put the top on, using the ribbon ties to secure it at the back. Measure over your shoulder to the top edge of the cropped top at both back and front to find the length of strap. Use pins to mark the positions of where you want the straps. Add 1" (2.5 cm) to the strap measurement for turnings and cut two lengths of ribbon to this new measurement.

6 Take off the top and pin the ribbon straps in place, turning under each end by ½"(1 cm). Stitch the end of each strap securely in place.

Beadwork

Beads and sequins add extra sparkle and richness to garments, from glittering evening clothes to T-shirts. They also can be used creatively to highlight areas on embroidered pictures and hangings – for example, a single pearl bead looks wonderful in the center of a flower, or two flashing green sequins can suggest a cat's eyes. Use an ordinary sewing needle for beads with large holes and sequins. If, however, the beads have very small holes, you will need a fine beading needle.

BEADED MOTIFS

If you stitch beads closely together onto fabric and add a containing border, it is possible to trim the backing fabric away at the edges and use the motif as a decorative component.

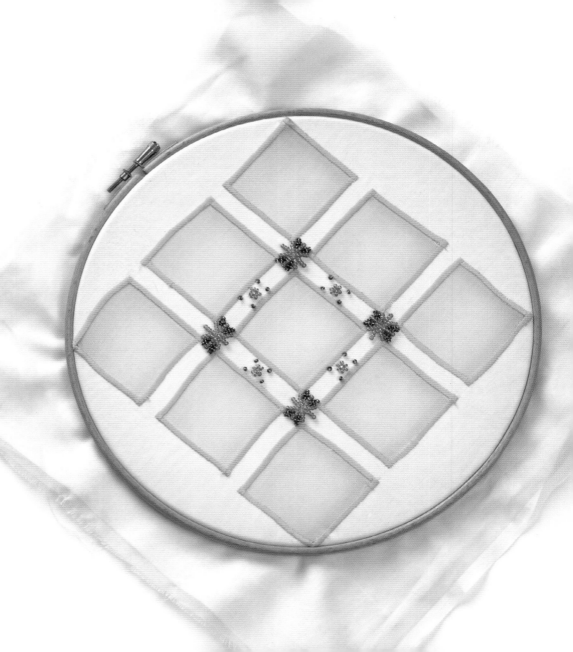

STITCHING BEADS

APPLYING INDIVIDUALLY
Bring out the needle and thread the bead. If the bead is round, insert the needle back through the same hole. With a long shaped bead, hold it down with your thumb and insert the needle close to its edge. Repeat.

COUCHING ROWS
Use two needles. Bring out the first needle and thread beads. Bring out the second needle close to the left of the first bead and make a small stitch over the thread. Slide next bead up, and repeat.

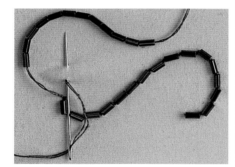

MAKING A FRINGE
Tie the first bead onto the thread, and knot securely. (If beads are large, start with a small bead.) Thread beads for one fringe strand; secure to the hem with a small backstitch. Repeat for each strand.

STITCHING SEQUINS

TWO-STITCH METHOD
This is used when securing one or more sequins. Use matching thread for almost invisible stitching or contrasting thread for a more decorative effect. Bring out the needle and thread the sequin. Make a backstitch over the right edge of the sequin and bring out the needle at the left edge. Stitch through the sequin again and repeat.

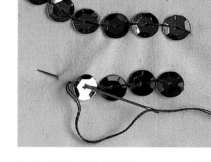

INVISIBLE STITCHING
Bring out the needle and thread on the sequin. Make a stitch over the sequin's left edge; place a second sequin so that its right edge covers the eye of the first. Bring out the needle at the left edge of the second sequin and insert the needle in its eye.

SECURING SEQUINS WITH BEADS
Bring out the needle; thread on a sequin and a bead. Insert the needle through the sequin eye and pull the thread so that the bead holds the sequin in place. Bring out the needle at the position for the next sequin.

BEADED EVENING WRAP

Decoratively patterned silk fabrics are widely available and can be transformed into glamorous wraps by adding glass beads and fringes, which catch the light beautifully. A floral design will allow you to add clusters of beads to the flower centers, or use your creativity to embellish the pattern of your choice.

You will need

- 2 yards (1.8 m) turquoise blue embroidered silk fabric, any standard width

- 2 yards (1.8 m) of dark blue silk fabric, any standard width

- glass beads of two contrasting shades

- beaded braid to tone with fabric, twice the length of the fabric width

MAKING THE WRAP

1 Use clusters of three beads to highlight areas of the design. Then stitch bead clusters of another color in the center of each flower. Beginning at the central cluster and radiating out along the center of each petal, couch lines of five beads of another color.

2 Place the beaded fabric and plain fabric right sides together. Pin and machine stitch down the two long sides, about ½" (1 cm) from the edges. Turn right sides out.

3 Fold under ½" (1 cm) on each of the short open ends; pin.

4 Baste around the entire circumference of each end, about ⅜" (8 mm) away from the edge.

5 Carefully insert the beaded fringe between the basted edges. Slipstitch the folded edges of the fabric to the braid on both sides, allowing a little of the braid to show at the edge.

TIP

It is a good idea to stretch the embroidered fabric in a hoop. This makes the fabric easier to handle and leaves both hands free for threading the beads.

BEADED BEACH BAG

Any plain straw bag can be transformed into designer chic by adding some ribbon, buttons, beads, and bows. It's so simple and inexpensive, you can treat yourself to a new look every year.

You will need

- Straw beach bag

- 1½" (3.5 cm) wide ribbon cut to the circumference of the top of the bag plus 1" (2.5 cm) for turnings

- Short lengths of narrow ribbon

- Stranded embroidery floss

- A selection of beads

- Small flower-shaped buttons

1 Starting at the back, lay the ribbon along the edge at the top of the bag with the ends extending about ½" (1 cm). Sew the ribbon to the inside of the bag or the liner, securing it about ½" (1 cm) down from the top inside edge. To make a neat edge, turn under the extending ends of the ribbon. Then secure the ribbon to the front of the bag with a line of stitching at the top and bottom of the ribbon.

2 Thread a needle with 2 strands of matching embroidery floss and stitch the beads to the bag evenly along the ribbon edge.

3 Using a strong thread, make 2 large and 1 small ribbon flowers (see box) and secure to the bag with a few stitches to the loops. Thread a large bead onto the center and secure with a small bead.

4 Create 3-bead clusters and stitch to the bag. Then scatter small flower-shaped buttons, securing them, as above, with large and small beads.

MAKING A RIBBON FLOWER

Take a short length of narrow ribbon and curl it around in a circular fashion, 1 loop at a time. Secure with a few stitches as you go. This will be the back of the flower.

DEALING WITH A LINING

If the bag is already lined, stitch the ribbon to the lining at the top. However, you should only stitch the ribbon flowers, bead clusters, and buttons to the bag. To have access to the inside of the bag, unpick the bottom seam of the lining and roll it back. When you've finished with the exterior decoration, slipstitch the lining back in position.

BEADED ESPADRILLES

Plain cotton espadrilles are easy to embellish with beads and sequins. The fabric is firm enough to carry the weight of the beads, yet soft enough to allow a needle to be pushed through without undue effort.

You will need

- Pair of espadrilles

- Matching sewing thread

- Pink and red sequins

- Pink glass beads

Whatever color your shoes, choose beads and sequins that stand out from the base fabric. On a blue espadrille, for example, you could try aqua and green.

MAKING THE SHOES

1 Enlarge the template below or cut your own heart shape out of paper or card to fit in the center of your shoes. Draw around it onto the fabric using a light colored pen or pencil.

2 Start by sewing on a row of overlapping sequins, following the outline of the heart motif. Knot your thread and bring the needle and thread to the surface. Work a backstitch (see page 17) over the right edge of the first sequin into the eye, then bring out the needle at the left edge and through the eye of the next sequin, placed edge to edge with it. Work another backstitch through the eye of the first sequin then bring the needle out to the left of the second sequin to thread the third sequin. Continue until all the sequins are secured.

3 Stitch 3 larger sequins inside the heart shape, securing each with stitches threaded through the center.

4 Fill in the remaining space with round glass beads. Thread a bead on to your thread and insert needle into the fabric close to the bead's edge before bringing needle to the surface close by to attach the next bead.

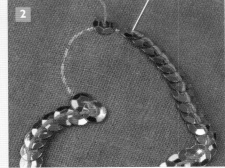

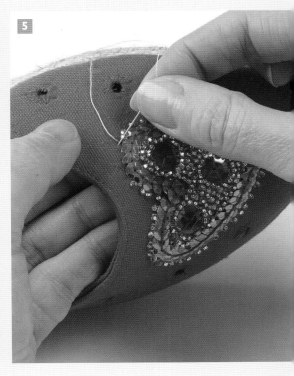

5 Finally, add a border of beads around the outside of the heart shape.

NOTE

In order to sew the beads and sequins in place you will need to employ a little dexterity, maneuvering fingers and needle inside the shoe. Wear thimbles to protect your fingers and keep the design away from the tip of the toe, where it is more difficult to stitch.

TEMPLATE

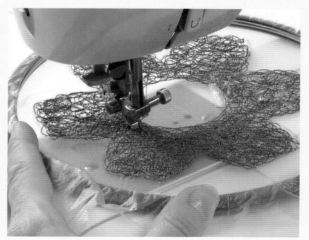

MACHINE EMBROIDERY

Using a simple machine, you easily can stitch decorative borders and motifs on garments and linens but, using the step-by-step instructions in this chapter, you also can make freehand designs that will let you produce embroidered scenes or create items solely from thread. Seven great projects are included to help you practice your machine skills while making some wonderful things to wear or use.

For machine embroidery it is essential to have an electric sewing machine with a foot pedal, which leaves both hands free to manipulate the fabric. The machine does not have to be complicated; the most basic swing needle (zig-zag stitch) machine is all you need to complete any of the projects in this book. Make sure you are familiar with the way your own machine works, how to operate its various controls, alter tension, and so on.

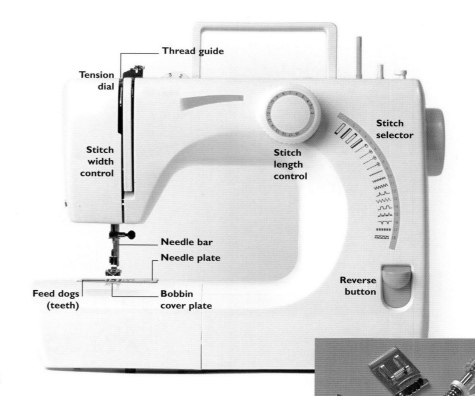

Thread guide
Tension dial
Stitch width control
Stitch selector
Stitch length control
Needle bar
Needle plate
Reverse button
Feed dogs (teeth)
Bobbin cover plate

TEETH OR FEED
In normal stitching mode, the teeth, which are alongside the needle plate, automatically feed the fabric under the needle. When darning or free stitching, you need to move the fabric in various directions so these teeth must be disconnected or lowered.

MACHINE NEEDLES
Standard needles are labeled with US, British, and continental sizes. For most sewing purposes, using medium-weight fabrics, a 12-80 or 14-90 is suitable but for embroidery, a thicker needle, such as a 16-100, is preferable. If you are not sure which needle to use, practice on a spare scrap of fabric.

Ballpoint needles are used when stitching synthetics and jersey fabrics.

Jeans needles have a tapered shape and very sharp point for penetrating tough denim fabrics, and are useful for embroidering on heavy fabrics or multiple layers.

MACHINE FEET
A presser foot is the standard foot used for most straight and zig-zag stitching. Choose an open-toe presser foot (top left), which has a "window" of transparent plastic – or is sometimes made entirely of transparent plastic. This allows a good view of stitches in progress.

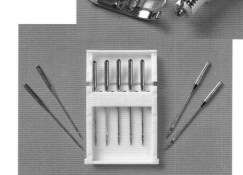

A darning foot (top right), sometimes known as a quilting foot, depending on the manufacturer, has a spring that enables it to move smoothly over uneven surfaces and allows flexible movement for stitching in different directions.

A cording foot (top middle) is used for couching threads or cords, with a groove ensuring that the cord is fed through into the correct position for the needle to stitch over it.

MACHINE THREADS

Ordinary sewing thread is good to experiment with when you are embarking on machine embroidery for the first time. But you will soon want to use some of the more unusual threads specially designed and manufactured for machine embroidery. Also, embroidery threads are often finer and more loosely twisted than mercerized sewing thread, and the fibers have better covering properties.

Cotton and polyester embroidery threads behave well with most machine techniques, both with set stitches and freehand embroidery. Look out for matt threads, shiny threads, variegated shades, and even fluorescent colors. Threads made from blended fibers tend to be stronger and less likely to break.

Rayon threads (above right) offer a subtle, silky sheen. Look for variegated colors and threads that are so shiny they look almost pearlescent. These speciality threads tend to be slightly more expensive that ordinary sewing thread so you may wish to economize by using a less expensive thread of a similar weight and thickness in the bobbin.

Metallic threads (above left)include types that appear almost to be made of pure spun gold or silver to those which are blended with other threads to produce a more subtle sparkle or glitter. Some metallic threads are easier to work with than others and you will need to experiment to find the ones you like best.

LINING, INTERFACING, AND OTHER SUPPORTS

 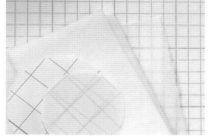

When it comes to embroidery there are easy fabrics and there are "difficult" ones such as very lightweight and sheer fabrics, velvet, lace, and silks, which will require some kind of support or reinforcement before you start to stitch.

You can use a firm, closely-woven fabric such as calico or linen as a backing, or one of the special materials designed for the purpose.

Interfacing (above right)is available in various weights and in fusible (iron-on) and non-fusible versions. One that is printed with a grid is useful when measuring and cutting.

Bonding web is a double-sided fusible interfacing invaluable in machine appliqué as it will fix one fabric to another. Medium and heavyweight bonding webs attach fabrics without the need for stitching, while lightweight webs, which are softer and more flexible, are usually used in association with stitching and are more suitable for delicate fabrics.

Stabilizers are non-woven materials which look and feel similar to interfacing and are used as a support under an area of hand or machine embroidery or appliqué. Some of these have an adhesive backing, protected by a layer of paper, while others are usually basted in place and the excess torn away after the stitching is completed.

Vanishing fabrics (above left)are usually used alone to create machine lace but have their uses as a backing for delicate, sheer, or fragile fabrics, too.

Machine stitches

Each of the projects in this book can be completed using the most basic sewing machine provided that it has a swing needle – meaning that it can produce a zig-zag stitch. There is no need for a sophisticated machine though, if you have one, you may enjoy substituting other stitches for the ones shown on a particular project.

Achieving decorative effects using set stitches is easy. In most instances, your sewing machine can be set up as for normal sewing. Before embarking on any new project, however, it is a good idea to practice the stitches on a spare piece of fabric, in case minor adjustments need to be made to stitch tension. Sewing a sample of each stitch will also help you to decide upon the appropriate width and length to which you should set the dials on your machine.

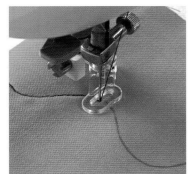

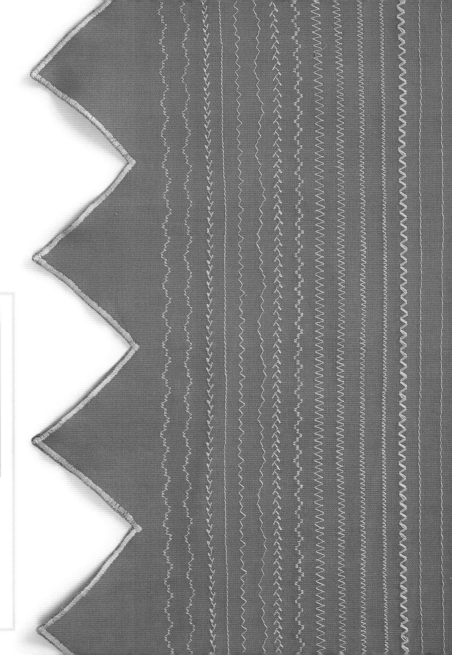

TENSION
Thread tension will affect the quality and appearance of your stitches. As a general rule, if the upper tension is too tight, "locks" (loops of thread) will appear on the surface of the fabric so you will need to decrease the tension. If the tension is too loose, locks will appear on the reverse, so increase the tension. Check your machine's instruction manual for tips on adjusting tension.

QUILTING FOOT
Using this attachment – sometimes also referred to as a darning foot – will allow you more flexibility when stitching, making it easier to stitch in wavy lines and round shapes, not just in straight lines.

BASIC MACHINE EMBROIDERY STITCHES

STRAIGHT STITCH

This is the basic sewing machine stitch and, while it is most often used for seams, it also can create decorative lines. When used for freestyle embroidery (see page 76), straight stitch can be made to produce a very different effect.

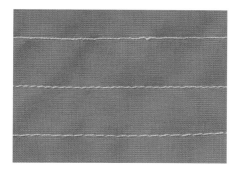

ZIG-ZAG STITCH

By altering the stitch length and width dials, you can produce lots of variations on the basic zig-zag, from an open pattern (top) to a closed "satin stitch" (bottom).

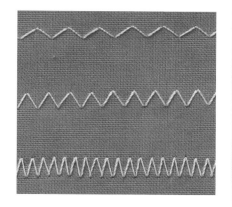

STRAIGHT STITCH VARIATION

Simply by crossing lines of straight stitch, you can create interesting patterns, either random or more formally arranged. This is also a useful device for quilting two or more layers of fabric.

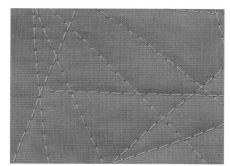

ZIG-ZAG STITCH VARIATION

By altering the width of a close zig-zag as you stitch, you can create some interesting effects. (Some machines produce this stitch pattern automatically.)

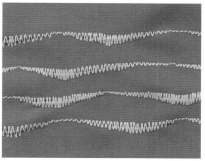

HERRINGBONE

If your machine has this stitch, use it directly on the fabric as surface decoration or to hold down the edges of ribbons and braids. It's also good around the edges of appliqué shapes. You may be able to vary the width and length of the stitch, which will produce different effects.

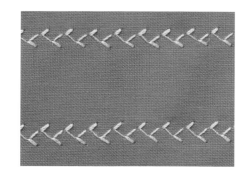

LIGHTNING STITCH

A widely available stitch choice (check your manual). Your machine may produce a similar stitch, or the same stitch with a different name. This is useful for decorative borders and to hold down the edges of ribbons and braids.

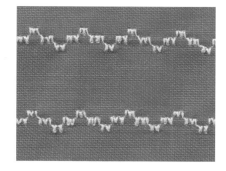

Designing for a machine

Most designs – apart from the simplest lines of decorative stitching or couching – will require some planning and will involve transferring the outlines of a design onto the fabric before you start to stitch. It's also important to consider the suitability of your design; frequently washed items, for example, need firm and flat stitches while little-worn or purely decorative items can take looser stitches and beads.

Machine embroidery, when thickly applied, tends to distort the fabric, so you may also need to use stabilizing or interlining materials (see page 65).

Some fancy threads, especially metallics, are more difficult to work with than others, so start with blended threads and progress to the more unusual types when you have gained confidence. Experiment on scraps of fabric and use these experiments to help you come up with your final design.

PROBLEM SOLVING

If you use threads of different weights, you may need to adjust the tension. You will also need to be prepared for some problem-solving, as a heavier thread can cause a weaker one to break or tangle. A heavier thread or fabric will also require a thicker gauge of needle.

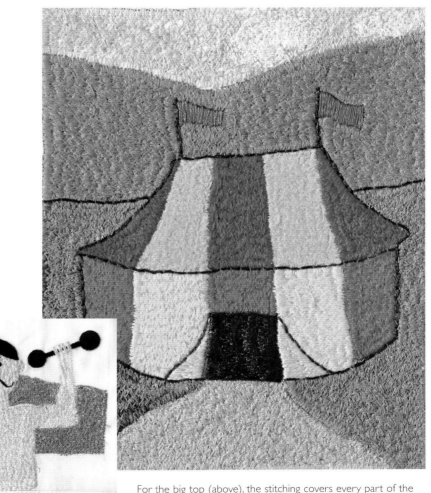

For the big top (above), the stitching covers every part of the fabric for a richly embroidered effect. For the strongman (left), areas of the design have been filled in with freestyle zig-zag stitches, leaving a background of unworked fabric.

PLANNING A DESIGN

TRANSFERRING DESIGNS

Several different methods are described on pages 14-15 and these are suitable also for machine embroidery. When using a stabilizing fabric, bonding web, or interlining, the design often can be drawn on this instead of on the actual fabric.

MEASURING

Each of the projects in this book includes a list of the materials needed to complete the project. When customizing a project, however, or embarking on your own designs, you will need to work out how much fabric, thread, or other materials you will need. When measuring, always remember to add generous seam allowances; this also applies if the fabric is to be stretched in a hoop or frame.

STITCH CHOICE

Before embarking upon a project, work some sample stitching on a spare piece of the fabric you will be using. This will help to determine whether the stitch is suitable for the fabric, and whether or not the tension, or the width or length of the stitch needs to be adjusted. It is also an opportunity to practice the stitch, to give you more confidence, especially when tackling a new technique for the first time.

SAMPLES

Keep any stitch samples or other experiments. They are a useful reference. You may also be able to incorporate some of them into future projects, or turn them into greetings cards.

THREAD CHOICE

If you are new to machine embroidery, start by using the same type of thread – preferably a standard sewing thread or a plain machine embroidery thread – in both the needle and the bobbin. As you gain confidence, you can experiment with different thread combinations and you will discover which threads are easiest and most difficult to use.

FABRIC CHOICE

For set stitches, almost any fabric can be used, though evenly woven cottons and linens are the easiest to work with, especially for a beginner.

For freestyle embroidery, you must have a firm, stable base. Medium to heavy fabrics made from natural fibers such as cotton, linen, and silk are the best. Really firm fabrics can sometimes be used without any kind of support but, as a general rule, the fabric should be stretched in a hoop. With fine fabrics, you may need to use more than one layer or back the fabric with a stabilizer or support.

Shiny or synthetic fabrics are the most difficult to work with. Synthetics are liable to tear, shiny fabrics to slip, and stretchy fabrics to distort.

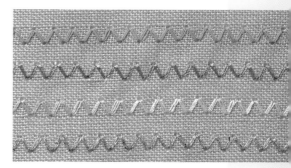

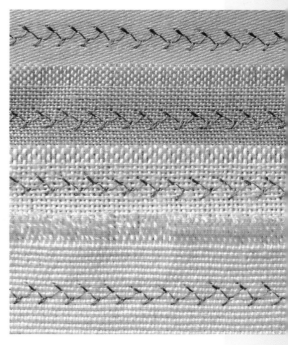

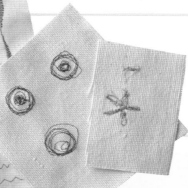

A machine embroidered border can be as simple as a line of topstitching along a hem or a zig-zag stitch holding a length of cord in place. Utilize the stitches your machine can produce in a creative way — and incorporate other materials such as lace, ribbons, braids, cords, and fabric strips — and you can create a range of border designs quickly and easily with the minimum of effort but the maximum impact.

SCALLOPED EDGE

If your machine offers this scalloped satin stitch effect as an option, you can use it to produce a fancy edging. Thread the top and bottom with the same thread and make sure the stitch is set to form a close zig-zag. The fabric should be trimmed close to the stitching — but take care not to cut any of the threads.

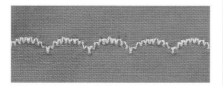

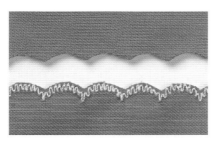

By using the most basic set stitches to hold down ribbons and cords of various widths and materials, you can create richly textured borders.

HOW TO CREATE SIMPLE BORDERS

USING STRAIGHT STITCH

Straight stitch is not just for sewing seams: it can be decorative in its own right. Stitch lines of straight stitch directly on to your fabric, or pin and baste a length of ribbon and use straight stitch to hold it in place.

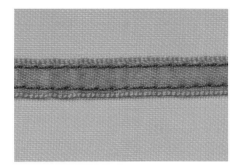

USING ZIG-ZAG STITCH

Once again, lines of zig-zag can be very decorative but they also have a practical application in holding down the edges of a length of ribbon or braid. Use a thread color to match the ribbon for a subtle effect, or a contrast color for greater impact.

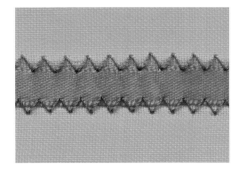

USING FANCY STITCHES

The variety of stitches at your disposal will depend on the type and sophistication of the sewing machine you are using – but even the most basic machine nowadays offers some fancy stitches, which can produce highly decorative borders used alone or with lengths of pretty ribbon.

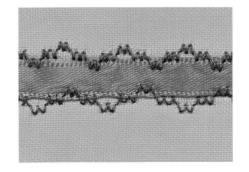

COUCHING LINES OF CORD

Use a basic zig-zag stitch and standard presser foot to hold down a length of cord. Set the stitch width so that the needle goes into the fabric at either side of the cord. This method can be used to place a cord along the edge of a piece of fabric, or for creating straight lines of couching.

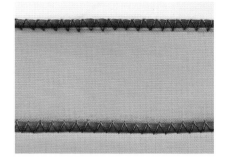

COUCHING WITH A SPECIAL FOOT

Using a special cording foot allows more flexibility, as the cord – or sometimes two or more cords at a time – are fed through the grooves and trapped by stitches as you go along. The diameter of the groove will limit the thickness of the cord that can be fed through, but it still allows you the freedom to use a variety of cords, including thick metallic threads, and 6-stranded embroidery threads (as shown here). With a cording foot, you can move the fabric quite freely as you stitch, so this method can be adapted to create wavy, looped, or zig-zag borders. To hold down the cord, use a matching or contrasting thread to create various different effects.

BORDERED HAND TOWEL

Embroidery is a great way to embellish plain fabrics. Here, a border of crisp white cotton fabric is decorated with lines of machine stitching and applied to a terrycloth hand towel.

You will need

- 16" (40 cm) white cotton fabric, at least 23" (57 cm) wide

- Cotton thread in white, blue, red, and green

- Hand towel, 22" (55 cm) wide

TIP
The instructions are for a border to fit a hand towel 22" (55 cm) wide but you can easily adapt this project to fit a towel of any width. The border would also look very pretty on other items: the edge of a curtain, tablecloth, or pillowcase, for example.

MAKING THE TOWEL

1 Cut a strip of white fabric measuring 23" × 4" (57 × 10 cm) and six 4" (10 cm) squares. Fold each square in half, then fold in the corners so that the short raw edges line up with the long raw edges. Press. Fold in ½" (1 cm) all around on the long strip, then fold the strip in half lengthways. Press.

2 With white thread in the top and bottom of the machine (blue thread is used here to show up the stitching), zig-zag down the center of each triangle to hold the folded edges in place.

3 Pin the 6 triangles, evenly spaced, along one folded edge of the strip.

4 Fold the other edge over, pin, and baste. Stitch along one short edge of the strip, then along the folded edge, and up the other short edge, about ⅛" (3 mm) from the fold.

5 With blue thread on top, straight stitch close to the zigzag edge then stitch close to the border's top edge.

6 Change to herringbone or other patterned stitch and make a line of stitching down the center of the border.

7 Change the top thread to red and stitch 2 more rows of herringbone (or your chosen stitch) either side of the line of blue, going in the opposite direction. Follow these with lines of zig-zag stitch in green.

8 Press the border, then slipstitch to the edge of the towel.

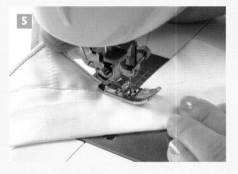

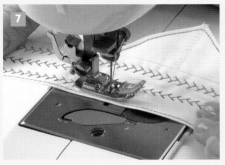

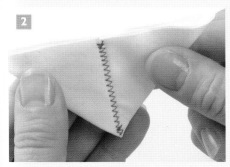

A plain skirt becomes something much more special if you apply a decorative border. Silk and velvet ribbons of different materials, lines of decorative stitching, and appliqué motifs are all easy to apply.

You will need

- Plain linen skirt

- 3 lengths of ½" (1 cm) ribbon, 1 velvet and 2 satin, each slightly longer than the circumference of the skirt

- Matching sewing thread

- Contrasting sewing thread

- Scraps of lightweight fabric and iron-on interfacing

Decorative trims
As well as ribbon of different textures and widths, lengths of lace and beading also could be used.

MAKING THE SKIRT

1 Pin the first ribbon in place about 1" (2.5 cm) from the lower edge of the skirt. Pin 2 more lengths of ribbon in a similar way, spacing them evenly apart.

2 Baste all 3 lengths in place.

3 With matching thread, stitch along both edges of the first ribbon, using a medium straight stitch. Stitch the other 2 ribbons in the same way, using matching thread as needed.

4 Add lines of feather stitching between the ribbons in a contrasting color to the skirt. You could vary the stitches using herringbone or zig-zag, depending on your sewing machine (see pages 70-71), or the number of lines used.

5 Finish with a line of decorative stitching above the top ribbon.

6 Trace the flower motif onto a scrap of fabric. Iron on interfacing to the back and stiffen the fabric. Using a close zig-zag stitch and contrasting thread, stitch around the edge of the flower. Place a small circle of a contrasting fabric in the center and close zig-zag around this. Stitch radiating lines out from the central circle. When finished, cut around the design, close to the stitching. Make a second flower motif in the same way.

7 Pin the first motif in place, using it to cover the joins in the ends of the ribbons. Slipstitch around the edge to secure. Pin the second motif in position at a different point around the bottom; slipstitch in place over the ribbons.

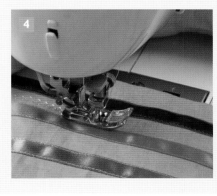
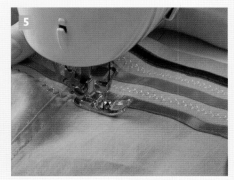

TEMPLATE

Using your sewing machine to create freestyle patterns opens up a world of new possibilities. Once you have got to grips with the small adjustments you need to make to your machine, and you have practiced the techniques on a few spare scraps of fabric, you will be able to move on to more ambitious projects.

The main difference between set stitching and freestyle is that the feed dogs, which usually move the fabric as you stitch, are lowered or covered so that you are free to move the fabric as you wish, in any direction.

Another difference is that you may choose to remove the foot altogether, or to replace the standard presser foot with one suitable for embroidery. Check the accessories that are supplied with your machine: there may be a darning foot, quilting foot, or embroidery foot. You will recognize it by the spring mechanism on the needle bar, which allows the foot to move smoothly over uneven fabrics but it has a small ring through which the needle enters the fabric and which exerts a little pressure on that small area of fabric immediately under the needle. For novices, the foot also offers some protection to your fingers.

Before you start to stitch, set the stitch type to straight stitch or zig-zag and the stitch length to zero. The zig-zag width can be altered according to the effect you wish to achieve: you can decide this by stitching on a small sample of fabric before you embark on a bigger project.

In this example, freestyle zig-zag is used to cover the background fabric completely, resulting in a richly embroidered effect that is quick and easy to achieve — even for a relative beginner.

HOW TO CREATE FREESTYLE EMBROIDERY

1 Remove the presser foot. You can replace it with a quilting or darning foot, if you wish, or simply leave it off.

2 Lower the feed dogs. Check your manual to see how to do this.

3 If your machine does not allow you to lower the feed dogs, cover them with self-adhesive tape.

4 Draw your design on the fabric. You can draw shapes freehand, use a template (as shown), or any of the methods described on page 15.

5 Stretch the fabric in an embroidery hoop. If the fabric is very thin or unstable, you may need to back it with one of the materials described on page 65.

6 Place the fabric flat on the bed of the machine, and lower the drop feed lever. Insert the needle, then lift it and draw the lower thread through to the surface.

7 Hold both threads as you begin to stitch. After you have made a few stitches, snip off the thread.

8 Move the fabric back and forth and from side to side as you stitch, holding the edges of the hoop. In this case, the stitch used is straight stitch.

9 This method can also be used with zig-zag stitch. Once again, make a few initial stitches before snipping off the thread ends.

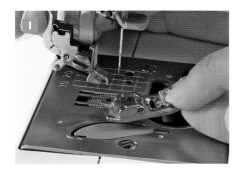

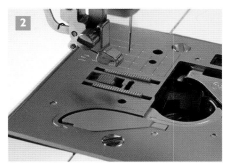

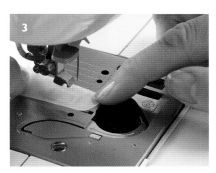

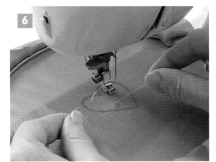

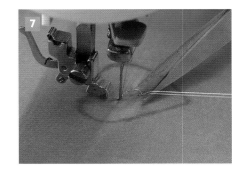

Machine embroidered fabrics

As well as being used to decorate fabrics, machine embroidery can be used to create new fabrics. You simply need to use a special material to support the stitching that is afterward removed completely from the finished work. Start with a small, manageable project such as the corsage on page 82. As you become more accomplished, you will be able to create fabrics ranging from wispy, gossamer-like lace to more robust pieces – and have great fun in the process.

Using one of a number of special fabrics, see below, you can build up a network of interlocking stitches that produce a lacy effect. It is essential that the stitching should overlap.

The special fabrics used for this method are available from most shops that sell embroidery materials and fall into three basic types.

Cold water-soluble materials – available in a variety of types, resembling fine netting, film, fabric, or paper, these are ideal for very fine work and are the most commonly available. Being transparent, it is easy to see the stitches being created as you work. Cold water soluble film has been used for the projects in this book.

Hot water-soluble film, which is

stronger and stiffer, can be worked without using a frame. It has the texture and appearance of fine silk and tends to be more expensive than the cold water type but is only suitable for use with threads that are colorfast and that can stand up to very hot water.

Vanishing muslin is a loose-weave fabric which, when heated, disintegrates. It is quite stiff, allowing it to be worked without the use of a hoop, but it is also quite brittle and produces a dust when heated that can be an irritant.

HOW TO CREATE MACHINE LACE FABRICS

1 Draw your design on a piece of vanishing fabric. Stretch the fabric in a hoop.

2 Lower the drop feed lever, insert the needle, lift it and draw the lower thread through to the surface. Hold both threads as you begin to stitch.

3 After you have made a few stitches, snip off the thread ends close to the fabric, then carry on stitching, moving the hoop in circular motions, and making sure that you create a network of overlapping stitches.

4 When you are satisfied that the piece is finished, and that the lines of stitching are all interlinked, remove the vanishing fabric according to the manufacturer's instructions (for example, by dissolving it in cold water).

5 Once you have finished stitching, excess vanishing fabric can be trimmed away. Keep these small pieces as they can be used again for other projects, to mend tears, or to reinforce small areas of stitching.

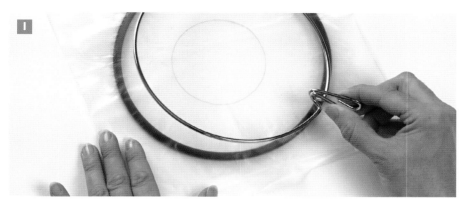

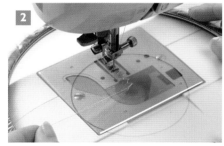

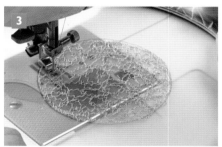

VANISHING FABRICS

When using vanishing fabrics for the first time, you are advised to use cold water soluble fabric which is the least expensive and most readily available. Most types resemble a sheet of plastic, and must be stretched in a hoop. Begin stitching with a fine-gauge needle and thin thread and move the fabric smoothly as you sew, as jerky movements will invariably cause the material to tear. Any tears, small or large, can, however, be repaired by laying another piece of the material under the hole and proceeding to stitch. Once you are confident about using the fabric, you can experiment with different threads.

TIP

It is important to remember that, when stitching on any vanishing fabric, the lines of stitching must overlap and connect or, when the support is removed, the stitching will ravel.

TOTE WITH PICTURE POCKET

Any plain or patterned bag can benefit from an extra pocket, in which to keep whatever needs instant accessing. Decorative embroidery can demonstrate the interests of the owner. Here, a pastoral scene enlivens a tote made from a dotted fabric.

You will need

- Scrap of unbleached calico or white cotton drill fabric

- Embroidery hoop

- White sewing thread

- Rayon machine embroidery thread, in pale blue, brown, and 3 shades of green

- Tiny flower-shaped buttons

- 8" × 7¾" (20 × 18 cm) piece of medium-weight denim fabric

- Cotton or canvas bag

TEMPLATE

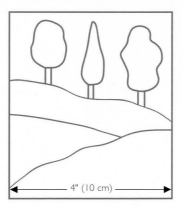

4" (10 cm)

MAKING THE TOTE

1 Enlarge the design as necessary and trace it on to a square of unbleached calico (or cotton drill). Stretch the fabric in a hoop. Place the hoop and fabric on the machine.

2 Thread the bobbin with ordinary white sewing thread and the needle with machine embroidery thread. The thread length should be set to 0, the thread width to medium, and the stitch to zig-zag; lower the feed dogs.

3 Start with pale blue and fill in the sky. Change the top thread to brown and fill in the tree trunks. Change the top thread to pale green and fill in one tree shape and the grass (and so on, until the whole design has been filled in).

4 When finished, remove from the machine and hoop. Sew on a selection of the buttons using green thread.

5 Trim the fabric very close to the sewing to leave a border approximately ⅟₁₆" (2 mm) all around.

6 Pin and baste the embroidered piece to the center of the denim. Use a medium width, close zig-zag stitch to attach the embroidered piece to the fabric, making sure you cover the

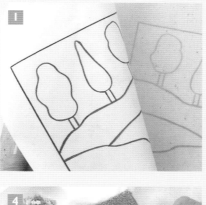
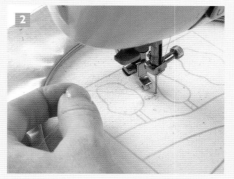

trimmed edges of the calico with your stitching on all sides.

7 Fold under the denim ¼" (5 mm) on all edges; fold twice to form a neat hem on the top edge; press. Slipstitch the top edge. This forms the pocket.

8 Pin and baste the pocket to the bag, positioning it centrally on the front of

the bag. Hand sew the pocket firmly in place around 3 sides, using straight stitch.

NOTE

Be prepared to rethread the bobbin with white thread several times when embroidering this design, as this technique uses a lot of thread.

A useful accessory for adding interest to coats, sweaters, and shawls, this lacy "flower" is created solely with machine-made stitching. Use a safety or dressmaker's pin to attach it to your garment.

You will need

- Water-soluble embroidery film

- Medium and small embroidery hoops

- Rayon machine embroidery thread in violet, deep pink, and turquoise

- Gold metallic machine embroidery thread

- 1½" (4 cm) self-covering button

- Self-adhesive water-soluble embroidery film

- Scraps of pink narrow ribbon and metallic cord

TIP

When cutting away excess film, do not discard it, as it can be used for other projects. Even the tiniest scraps can be useful for mending tears that may appear in the fabric while stitching.

MAKING THE CORSAGE

1 Draw a flower shape (see page 78) on to water soluble embroidery film and stretch the film in a hoop.

2 Thread the bobbin with violet thread and the needle with deep pink. Lower the feed dogs and remove the foot. Set the stitch length to 0 and the stitch type to straight stitch. Place the hoop under the needle and lower the needle lever. Bring the bobbin thread to the top of the work and, holding both threads in one hand, lower the needle into the fabric and make the first few stitches by turning the wheel manually.

3 Holding the hoop lightly with both hands, proceed to stitch slowly, rotating the hoop to create overlapping spirals of stitching. Continue until you have covered the whole pattern area with an interlaced cobweb of stitches.

4 Change the top thread to turquoise and stitch another network of threads over the top of the pink. Finally, add a lighter covering of gold stitches.

5 Remove the work from the hoop and trim off excess film. Make a second flower shape in exactly the same way.

6 Plunge the work into a bowl of cold water and agitate gently until the film has completely dissolved. Tease the work into shape and dry.

7 Cut a circle of self-adhesive film 3" (7.5 cm) in diameter and peel off the backing. Cut short lengths of ribbon and metallic cord and lay these across the adhesive film, then place this in the center of a square of dissolving film and stretch in a small hoop.

8 Place the hoop on the sewing machine and create spirals of stitching, as before. Trim off any excess fabric, dissolve the film, and dry the work. Use it to cover the button.

9 Run a gathering stitch around the center of one of the flowers and pull up to gather slightly, then slipstitch to the edge of the button. Do the same with the second flower, reversing it to create a contrast color.

RUFFLED SCARF

A pretty pink scarf is easy to create using a stretch-and-sew technique. The tasselled ends of the scarf are decorative and are an easy way to neaten the raw edges and add weight.

You will need

- 1½ yards (1.3 m) of stretch cotton jersey fabric, any width (fabric used here is 60" (1.5 m) wide

- Polyester thread in dark red

TIP

The fabric used here is a soft jersey. You need to choose a fabric with a certain degree of stretch, to create the wavy-edged effect. Jersey also drapes well, is soft to the touch, and creates a scarf that can be worn all year round, whatever the weather.

   The strip used to cover the join and form the top of the tassel may need to be slightly shorter or longer than the measurements given here, depending on how thick your fabric is, and how tightly you gather it.

MAKING THE SCARF

1 Cut a lengthwise strip of fabric measuring 1⅓ yards × 20" (1.2 m × 50 cm). Fold in half lengthways and draw a line down the fold using an erasable marker. Using this line as a guide, draw parallel lines 2¾" (7 cm) apart, 5 lines in all.

2 Thread the bobbin and the needle with red sewing thread, or the color of your choice. The thread length should be set to 0, the thread width to medium and the stitch to zig-zag. Start by stitching the two long edges of the scarf. Begin about 1½" (4 cm) from one end, to allow you to hold the fabric taut. Continue to stretch the fabric and allow it to fold over by about ⅛" (3 mm) as you sew, as this creates a neat wavy edge.

3 Fold along one of the lengthways lines you have drawn and stitch in the same way as the raw edges of the scarf, along the whole length, leaving about 1½" (4 cm) unstitched at each end. Repeat along the other lines.

4 Cut two 16" × 12" (40 × 30 cm) rectangles from the remaining fabric. Fold each rectangle in half (so that it measures 8" × 12" (20 × 30 cm) and place on a cutting mat. Using the lines of the mat as guides, cut strips ½" (1 cm) apart,

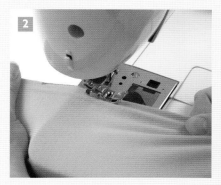

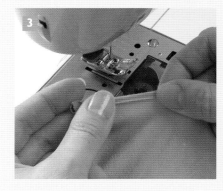
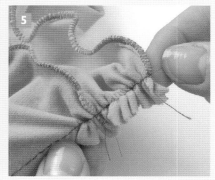
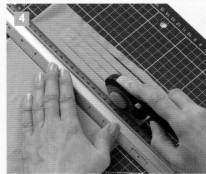
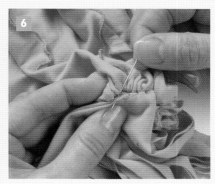

to form a fringe. Be careful to leave about 1½" (4 cm) uncut at the folded end.

5 Roll up the fringe and secure with a few stitches. Stitch a line of running stitches, by hand or machine, along each end of the scarf and pull up to gather.

6 Baste one fringed piece to each end of the scarf. Cut 2 strips of fabric, each measuring 12" × 4" (30 × 10 cm). Stitch the 2 short edges together to form a tube and fold in the raw edges so that they meet in the middle on the inside. Slip this tube over the join between the fringe and the scarf and slipstitch in place.

| TRINKET BOX

Create an eco-friendly storage unit by covering a small can with fabric and adding appliquéd machine-embroidered flowers. A silk lining will prevent items becoming scratched.

You will need

- ½ yard (45 cm) bright yellow medium-weight woven cotton fabric

- ½ yard (45 cm) pink silk or polyester lining

- Scraps of green silk or polyester lining

- Fusible bonding web

- Rayon machine embroidery thread in green, yellow, and variegated pink

- Yellow sewing thread

- Erasable pen

- Empty can, approximately 5" (12 cm) high and 4" (10 cm) in diameter; file down any rough edges

- Fluorescent orange beads

- Small scrap of ribbon

TEMPLATE

← 3½" (8.75cm) →

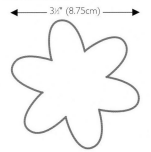

MAKING UP

Cut a rectangle measuring 13½" × 7¼" (34 × 18 cm) and a circle 4¾" (12 cm) in diameter from the yellow and pink fabrics; cut an extra circle from the pink lining fabric.

1 Trace 4 flower and 4 leaf shapes on to the backing paper of the fusible web. Cut roughly around each shape and apply the flowers to the pink fabric and the leaves to the green, using a hot iron, according to the manufacturer's instructions. Cut out around the drawn outline, peel off the backing paper, and apply 3 flowers and 4 leaves, evenly spaced, to the yellow fabric rectangle, and 1 flower to the center of the yellow fabric circle.

2 With yellow sewing thread in the bobbin and variegated pink embroidery thread in the needle, set the stitch width to medium and the stitch length between fine and 0. Then, starting at the base of one of the petals, embroider all around each flower. Pull stray lengths of thread to the back of the work and knot together, to neaten. Do the same with the flower on the lid.

3 Change the top thread to green and embroider around each leaf. Then, with an erasable marker pen, draw in stamens

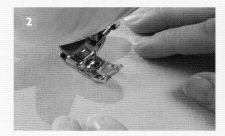

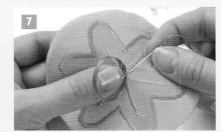

and stems freehand. Stitch the stems with green thread then change to yellow thread for the stamens. Stitch a cluster of beads in the center of each flower.

4 With right sides facing, stitch the side seam, about ½" (1 cm) from the 2 short edges, and turn right sides out. Stitch the side seam of the pink lining fabric, then stitch 1 of the circles to one end to form a base.

5 Slip the cover over the can and tuck under about ¾" (2 cm) at the bottom, to neaten. (Glue or stitch this hem in place, as you prefer.) Slip the lining inside the can.

6 Fold under the top edges of the main fabric and the lining, to correspond with the edge of the canister, then slipstitch the 2 folded edges together.

7 To make the lid, place the yellow and pink circles together, right sides facing, and stitch all around, ½" (1 cm) from the edge, leaving a small gap for turning. Clip all around, turn right sides out, tuck in the raw edges, and slipstitch the opening closed. Stitch a loop of ribbon and a few beads to the flower center.

This cover is the right size for a small crib, a Moses basket, or baby carriage. Made from squares of crisp cotton fabric, it is backed with plain fabric and interlined with lightweight batting for comfort and warmth. For a larger cover, increase the number of squares and cut the backing to the size you need, adding more star shapes to fit the larger area.

You will need

- Fat quarters or scraps of pink-on-white print cotton, white-on-pink print cotton, pink gingham, and pale pink gingham

- 1¼ yards (1 m) of plain cotton, at least 36" (90 cm) wide

- Scraps of yellow cotton fabric

- 10" (25 cm) of lightweight fusible bonding web, 36" (90 cm) wide

- Polyester or cotton thread to match fabric

- 1 yard (90 cm) lightweight batting

- 6 yards (3.6 m) pale blue bias binding, 1" (25 mm) wide

- Crewel needle

- Stranded embroidery floss in a contrasting color (or to match binding)

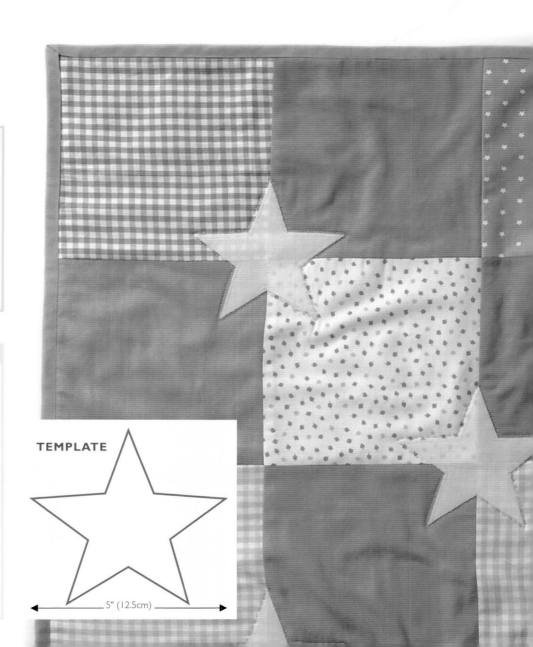

TEMPLATE

5" (12.5cm)

MAKING THE COVERLET

1 Cut the fabric into 8" (20 cm) squares, using a cutting mat, steel ruler, and cutting wheel for greater accuracy and speed. You will need 10 plain pink squares, 4 pink-on-white, and 2 each of the other 3 fabrics.

2 Join the patches in 4 rows of 5, with a ½" (1 cm) seam, following the chart for positioning. Press seams flat, then join the rows to form the front of the coverlet. Press seams flat.

3 Enlarge the star motif template as necessary. Make a tracing and use it to create a cardboard template. Place the star on the paper backing of the fusible bonding web and draw around it, using a pencil. Cut out roughly, place on the wrong side of the yellow fabric and bond, using a hot iron, according to the manufacturer's instructions.

4 Cut out along the pencil lines. Repeat step 3 to produce 6 stars. Peel off the paper backing and arrange the stars in place on the patchwork, at the intersections of the seams.

5 Thread the bobbin with pink or white thread and the needle with yellow, to match the stars. Set the thread length and width to medium and the stitch to

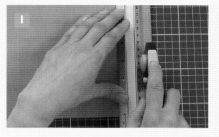

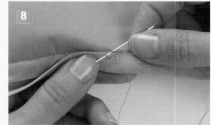

zig-zag. Stitch around each star shape, to hold it firmly in place.

6 Place the patchwork face up on the batting and backing fabrics, pin and baste all around, then cut off any excess so that all 3 layers are the same size.

7 Pin, baste, and machine stitch bias binding all around the front of the quilt, to neaten the edges.

8 Fold the binding over to the back and slipstitch by hand along the stitched line, mitering each corner neatly.

9 Finally, thread a crewel needle with two strands of embroidery floss and sew a decorative running stitch around each star, through all thicknesses of fabric. You may find it easier to use a hoop.

TIP
Fat quarters can be an economical way of buying a number of different fabrics for a project. These are fabric pieces offered by quilting retailers. A fat quarter will yield four 8" (20 cm) squares with only a little wastage.

The italic alphabet below is best enlarged (or reduced) as necessary and then traced on to transfer paper. The cross stitch letters are fifteen squares high.

Aa Bb Cc Dd Ee Ff Gg
Hh Ii Jj Kk Ll Mm Nn
Oo Pp Qq Rr Ss Tt Uu
Vv Ww Xx Yy Zz

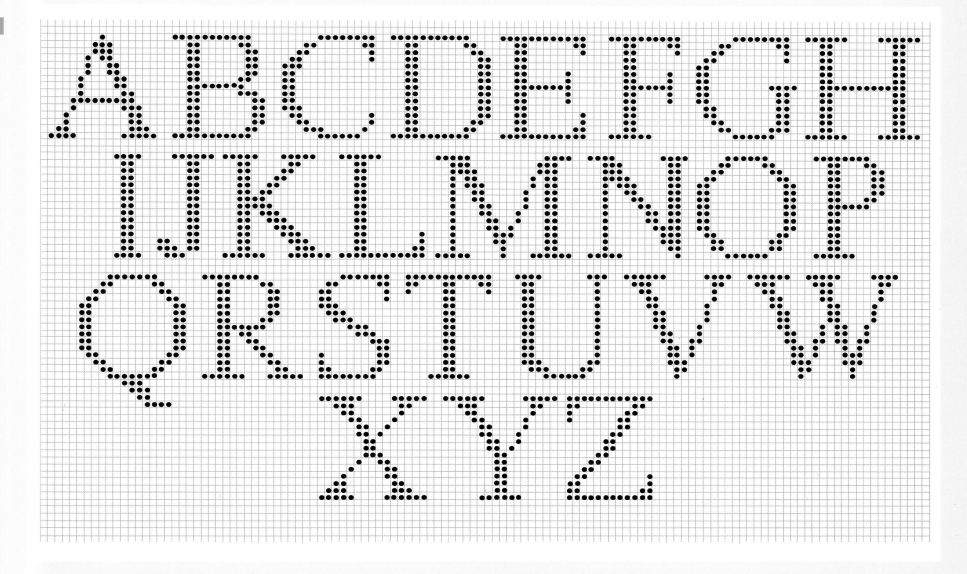

Once finished, most pieces of embroidery only require a light pressing on the wrong side of the background fabric. However, if the work has become badly distorted, it will need to be soaked and blocked to remove any creases and to ease it back into shape. If you plan on framing your work, it must first be mounted.

Regular inspection, a gentle hand wash, and careful storage will guard against dust, dirt, and moths. If the embroidery is delicate or is not colorfast, take it to a specialist rather than attempting to clean it yourself. Wash all embroideries very gently by hand in lukewarm water, using pure soap flakes or a mild detergent recommended for delicate fabrics. Do not rub the piece; rinse several times in lukewarm water until the water runs clear. End with a cold-water rinse. Most modern embroidery threads are colorfast, but you should still test them before washing (see box). If any dyes run, do not wash; dark colors and reds are the most likely to run. If the embroidery is lined, the lining should be removed and washed separately.

TESTING FOR COLORFASTNESS

Press a wet cotton ball against the threads and check for staining; alternatively, test scraps of the threads in hot water.

CARE TECHNIQUES

PRESSING

Place the embroidery, right side down, on a padded surface. Cover it with a damp or dry cloth (depending on the type of fabric used). With the iron at the correct setting for the fabric, press very gently all over. Never put an iron on the right side of an embroidered piece as it will flatten the stitches, and may scorch it.

BLOCKING

Check that the background fabric and the yarns will not run when wet (see page 92), otherwise the piece will have to be blocked dry.

1 Soak the embroidery in cold water, and roll it in a clean towel to remove the excess moisture.

2 Cover a soft board with plastic or cotton, and pin in position. Lay the embroidery on top of the covered board, right side up. Using steel pins, pin the piece at each corner, keeping the pins outside the area of work. Stretch the embroidery, and pin at 1" (2.5 cm) intervals, starting at the center. Leave pinned until completely dry.

MOUNTING

Hardboard should be cut to the same size as the work, or slightly larger to accommodate a cardboard mat or a frame with an edge.

1 Press the finished embroidery, and lay it right side down on a table. Center the hardboard on top, and turn the edges of the fabric to the back of the board.

2 Lace the edges together with strong thread, making evenly spaced stitches. Carefully pull the stitches tight, and secure with a few backstitches.

3 Fold and lace the side edges in the same way, pulling evenly so that the work is stretched smoothly.

> ### STORAGE
> If a piece is not in use, wrap it in plenty of acid-free paper and store flat, or roll it up with tissue paper. If it has to be folded, rearrange the piece from time to time so that the creases don't set. Check the embroidery for moths and mildew, and clean it when necessary.

Index

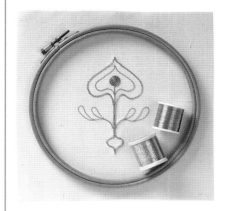

Acknowledgments

Projects created by:

Gwen Diamond

Lorraine Diamond

Sam Beresford

Hazel Arnott

Susie Johns

Cheryl Owen

Template maker:

Amanda Williams

For Carroll & Brown Limited:

Editorial	Amy Carroll
Design	Chrissie Lloyd
	Denise Brown
	Emily Cook
Production	Louise Dixon

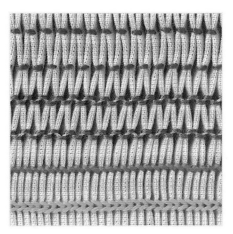